hipGRAPHIC KNITS

QUARRY

hipGRAPHIC KNITS

Unique Patterns and Techniques for Adding Stylish Graphics to Your Knitted Designs

Rochelle Bourgault and Lisa B. Evans

QUARRY BOOKS

✳ domestic arts for crafty girls

First published in the United States of America by
Quarry Books, a member of
Quayside Publishing Group
33 Commercial Street
Gloucester, Massachusetts 01930-5089
Telephone: (978) 282-9590
Fax: (978) 283-2742
www.rockpub.com

Library of Congress Cataloging-in-Publication Data
Bourgault, Rochelle, 1979-
    Hip graphic knits : unique patterns and techniques for adding stylish graphics to your knitted designs / Rochelle Bourgault and Lisa B. Evans.
        p.   cm. — (Domestic arts for crafty gals)
    ISBN 1-59253-262-4 (pbk.)
    1. Knitting—Patterns. I. Evans, Lisa B. II. Title.
TT825.B657 2006
746.43'2041—dc22

                                                                                    2006009188
                                                                                    CIP

ISBN-13: 978-1-59253-262-9
ISBN-10: 1-59253-262-4

10 9 8 7 6 5 4 3 2 1

Cover Design: Rockport Publishers
Design: Rockport Publishers
Production Design: Dutton & Sherman Design
Cover image and photography by Allan Penn
Technical editing and graphs by Sue McCain
Technique illustrations by Lorraine Dey, pages 136–139 (left); 143 (bottom right); 144–145
Illustrations by Judy Love, pages 139 (right); 140–143 (top and bottom, left), previously published in *1-2-3 Embroidery,*
    © 2001, Rockport Publishers, Inc.
Embroidery illustrations by Judy Love
Templates, page 127 (left) by Stewart Watkins

Printed in China

contents

Aztec Capelet, page 74

Star-Bellied Toddler Sweater, page 124

Graph This!

A Primer on Color Work

disclaimer: No reindeer, snowmen, pandas, or puppies were knit (or even sketched) in the creation of this book.

You've hunted far, wide, hither, and yon for a book that features all that *Hip Graphic Knits* offers. An abundance of pattern books feature chunky projects touted as simple and instantly gratifying. But how do you take knitting to the next level? Answer: Color. Patterns. Minimalism isn't the only thing that's hip, and patterns don't have to include teddy bears. We agree there is something to be said for fat needles and even fatter yarn: been there, done that. But without getting bogged down in technical details or knitting something so elaborate only your grandma would wear it, you can up your knitting's ante.

Imagine a farmers' market piled high with fresh fruit and vegetables. So many textures, sizes, and flavors to be sampled! So many enticing colors, smells, and tastes to be explored! Knitting with graphic color is really no different. It is exciting and stimulating to the senses. Think of it as cooking with a pair of needles and lots of irresistible fibers.

Graphic knitting is built upon one thing: a single stitch. If you can visualize it and you can graph it, then you can knit it. Whether it's a T-back tank, a pair of long, flirty gloves, or even a tea cozy, it can be broken down into a grid and knitted. No matter how big or small the project, for every stitch there is a square on a grid.

Our collection of contemporary graphic patterns for knitted garments, accessories, and home decor suits the tastes of even the most seasoned chick with sticks. *Hip Graphic Knits* will give you the knowledge you need to create a work of art. Knitting with color requires no specialized tools or rarified techniques. Stripes are just stripes, intarsia's bobbins and Fair Isle's stranding are simple concepts, and appliqué is working only on the surface of a finished garment. We've devoted an entire chapter to each of these techniques to broaden your skills and set your imagination free. In these pages, you will learn how to enhance, embellish, or overhaul a project that piques your interest but isn't quite right. If you're feeling bold, then go a step further and build an entirely new project around a color, shape, or texture that suits your own personal style.

This book is packed with sample palettes, color-drenched projects, step-by-step techniques, and illuminating sidebars. Every project includes a stitch-by-stitch graph, instructions, and ideas for personalization. The appendix features additional graphs that can be used in place of those in the featured projects. Knit them as they are or use them as inspiration for pieces you design yourself.

Ultimately, we want you to use *Hip Graphic Knits* to build your confidence and expand your skills. As Lisa's mother always said (and still does!), "You have to know the rules before you can break them." Use the tools we provide you—visualizing color combinations, planning smooth and stylish patterning, honing your knitting repertoire—to leap far beyond the simple stockinette stitch.

Today's fashion-savvy knitters are brimming with enthusiasm for fresh takes on the classics. And if you have read this far, then you must be one of them! So grab some needles and get graphic!

(And, if you happen to want a reindeer on your sweater, you'll learn how to design one yourself.)

Rochelle & Lija

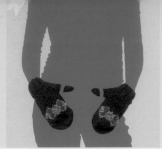

chapter

1

The Knitty Gritty of Color Knitting

Using This Book

We won't teach you how to knit in this book. We simply do not have the page real estate to illustrate casting on, the knit stitch, the purl stitch, binding off, and so on. We are assuming one of two facts to be true: (1) you know the knitting basics, and are looking to expand your repertoire and find inspiration, or (2) you have selected a companion volume that teaches the basics. The best way to hone your knitting skills, as with most skills, is by diving right in and challenging yourself.

That said, if you are a novice knitter, do not let the absence of the words *simple*, *beginner*, or *basic* from these projects dissuade you. Even the greenest knitter can apply colorwork techniques. If you can start a new ball of yarn in the middle of a row, then you can switch colors—and that is the first step to mastering graphic knitting.

As we will repeat throughout this book, there are two basic concepts that will help you immeasurably. First, color is spectacular. It adds zest to your life not to mention your projects. Second, graphs are essential to transferring designs—yours or ours—to your knitting.

Graphic Workshop

At first glance, graphs may seem intimidating. (What if I lose count? I'm supposed to knit with *how many* colors?) You don't have to be an accountant, or an engineer, to draw a graph. If you remember these basics, you will soon read graphs as easily as you read words on a page.

✳ Graphs represent the front (right side, or RS) of your knitted work. What you see is what you'll get.

✳ All right-side (RS) rows are numbered along the right-hand edge of the chart, and all wrong-side (WS) rows are numbered along the left-hand edge of the chart. RS rows are worked from right to left and WS rows are worked from left to right. The position of the "1" in the chart indicates where you start, whether on a RS row (see charts A and B on page 72) or WS row (see charts C and D on page 72). If the "1" is on the left edge, you start on a WS row; if it's on the right, you start on a RS row. When working in the round, you only have numbers along the right-hand edge, since all rows are RS rows. When working in the round, you always read from right to left, on every row.

✳ If you are knitting in the round (on double-pointed or circular needles), every row is worked from right to left.

✳ In both flat and circular knitting, a graph is read one row at a time, bottom to top, until all rows have been completed.

✳ If a pattern indicates "repeat 2 times," it simply means to knit across the entire row of stitches, and then do it again, before going on to the next line or row.

✳ One square equals one stitch. Instructions for knitting the first row of the graph below would read, "K7 in MC, switch to CC, k8, switch to MC, k to end." Note how the graph represents this.

✳ Most graphs (excluding the Gallery of Graphs, page 146) will have a legend that indicates color or stitch type using solid color boxes or symbols.

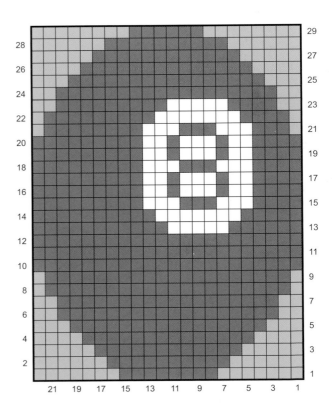

✱ A graph's size is independent of knitting gauge. It doesn't matter if you are knitting with size 3 or size 35 needles, or if your work is weighing in at a minuscule ten stitches per inch (2.5 cm) or a whopping two stitches per inch (2.5 cm). Every square in the graph is equal to one stitch.

✱ A graph's versatility is entwined with your chosen gauge. The fifty-two-stitch-wide Audrey Hepburn motif featured on page 135 would be a perfect motif for a roomy handbag, but would require being knit in some seriously fine yarn if you wanted Audrey Hepburn on your socks.

✱ The squares of a knitting grid are not true squares: they are rectangles that are slightly wider than they are tall. This bit of geometry is drawn from the fact that a knit stitch in stockinette stitch is slightly wider than it is tall. Creating your own graphs on quadrille-lined loose-leaf or engineering graph paper will create knit motifs that appear vertically compressed, unless you make allowances for this fact by enlarging the image or motif vertically by about 110 percent. The graphs in this book, as in most industry publications, consist of squares. (See page 157 for a page of knitter's graph paper that can be photocopied and used for projects of any gauge and scale.)

Matching Yarns to Projects

The yarns we used to create each project are listed in each pattern. You can purchase these yarns at your local yarn store, online if you can't find them in stock, or you can substitute another yarn for the ones recommended. Always knit up a gauge swatch to ensure that your yarn choice and needle size will produce the gauge required to knit the piece as designed.

Color and Design Basics

The basic color knitting techniques we discuss in this book are stripes, Fair Isle and stranding, intarsia, and the use of surface embellishments. Each technique's respective chapter outlines the differences among the styles, with illustrations that further illuminate the techniques. While we don't cover a course on design theory in the pages of this book, we can touch on some of the elements common to knitting design that you should keep in mind.

Texture, Color, Rhythm, Balance

Talk to any designer and she will recite to you the principles and elements of design that are constant across the discipline, not just to knitwear designers or fiber artists. Address and accommodate these issues and you will enjoy success in your efforts to create an exquisite piece that meets not only aesthetic standards but your personal vision.

Texture

Texture subtly dictates many of our day-to-day choices, from food to fabric. Are you a creamy or chunky peanut butter gal? More appropriately, are there yarns you gravitate towards without fail? Are you a sucker for velvety chenille, nubby wool blends, single-ply silk, or four-ply tweed? Acknowledging your preferences, and working with instead of fighting against them, will allow you to make satisfying decisions as you plan your projects. Opt for textures that please you and feel pleasant to the touch. Incorporate unexpected hints of texture by adding beads, bobbles, French knots, or ribbing to finish a piece.

Color

Color is like oxygen: it sustains good projects and allows them to thrive. Do you unconsciously surround yourself with the same colors, over and over again? Do you come home from a whirlwind shopping spree only to find that you've stockpiled yet another pink cardigan or orange scarf? These same instinctive color choices will help you navigate the yarn store as well.

You may need to strike a balance between the yarn colors in stock in a particular style of yarn and your unique vision for a project. Aching for a raspberry pink chunky wool-cotton blend, but finding it only in bubblegum? Find the color you want in a smaller gauge yarn, double it up, and no one will be the wiser.

When selecting multiple colors for a graphic knit project, keep the basics of color harmony in mind. Do all colors work together, or is there a color that seems out of place? Is a consistent value maintained, or is there a noticeable gap? Adding a dose of an unexpected but harmonious color is a hallmark of good design.

Lime-green lining fabric serves a practical purpose—adding durability to this messenger bag (see page 94)—but doubles as a clever piping detail.

Rhythm and Balance

The elements of texture and color are embedded in your yarn choices, whereas rhythm and balance are factors incorporated in your pattern that address the placement and repetition of a motif and colors. The entire work should be considered as a whole because where the eye is drawn is just as important as where it is not.

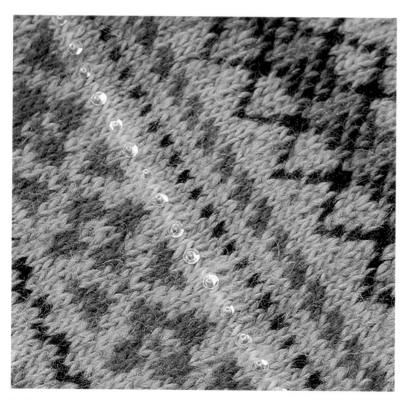

Iridescent sequins and seed beads stitched onto this Fair Isle cardigan (see page 68) are purely decorative, but demonstrate design savvy.

When you've selected a graph that you want to incorporate into a project, sketch a few ideas before you make a commitment. You may discover that your motif looks best in a place you never anticipated. Ask yourself, "What looks right? What looks best?" and the all-important, "Where will this motif be most visible?" You don't want to shortchange any of your design work by hiding the goods.

Does the placement of your design make sense and convey the idea or message you want it to convey? Many times, visual balance is determined intuitively, but sketches will weed out the less-than-perfect plans. The squared surfaces of the Tribal Sun Messenger Bag (see page 94) lend themselves well to a centered, relatively large motif. The Monogrammed Handbag (see page 44) is better suited to an off-centered graphic, as the letter is relatively narrow and might be overwhelmed by the background if centered. Not every design begs to be centered, but it's a good place to start the process.

Once you find a spot for your motif that pleases you, that is in line with your design vision, consider a second or repeated image. Would this improve on the overall design? The Pear Amour Leg Warmers (see page 90) and the Moon Day Yoga Tank (see page 120) are prime examples of projects that benefit from the rhythm of a repeated pattern. A project's stitch and row count are the only practical bounds limiting the repetition of a chosen graph. (After all, if you're buying yarn for one graph, you'll likely have enough for two or three, size and scale pending.) You may at some point need to pull out a calculator to finesse the final placement of your image and tweak the stitch count a little. For example, if you'd like a twelve-stitch-wide motif to tile across the entire width of a project, the project's stitch count should be a multiple of twelve, or a multiple of twelve with regular additional stitches between motifs or at the edges.

How to Choose a Color Combination

You are in the yarn store, having flashbacks to childhood—you are surrounded by jelly beans, wrapped licorice, and gummy sweet nothings. You want to fill your basket with lush skeins, hanks, balls, and cones of yarn, the raw materials of your version of creativity. But yarn is pricier and more precious than penny candy, and you're planning a sweater/scarf/hat/tea cozy for so-and-so's birthday, and you must be disciplined. You must narrow down your choices (if only temporarily), and (ominous drum-roll) select colors.

Though, in theory, the color palettes available to knitters know no bounds, the reality is that yarn options are determined by a season's or a year's fashion colors, and manufacturer's availability. Still, there are literally thousands of choices.

Planning a graphic knit and sticking to one brand and one line of yarn is a safe bet in many ways. The available palette has been professionally designed to have complementary and harmonious options, even if the number of colors available is not infinite. The colors will have comparable tonal strength, allowing for easy mixing and matching. Yarns from the same line also have identical weights and gauges, which ensures an even fabric.

The Limits of Shopping Online

Most yarn companies have websites that feature color swatches, lush descriptions, and patterns for sale. However, very few offer users the option of purchasing yarn online. It is often easiest to shop for ideas online, and then visit your local yarn or craft store to make your purchase.

When browsing for yarns online, keep in mind that, like snowflakes, no two computer screens will show colors exactly alike. A swatch of yarn on a website might look completely different in the store. If you know the manufacturer's shade number of the yarn color you desire, you can be reasonably assured that what you see in person will be what you want. Be careful, however, when purchasing more than one skein of a color, that the dye lot numbers match. While a difference in color may not be noticeable at the time of purchase, when the yarns are knitted together, the differences can be glaring.

How to Plan a Graphic Knit

Put simply, anything that can be drawn can be turned into a graphic knit. Any image that features color variations and discrete shapes or components is a good candidate for graphic interpretation.

Visualize, Brainstorm, and Sketch

Drink in the natural and material worlds, draw upon anything that catches your eye or piques your interest. You can have a specific project in mind, or not at all. The important thing is not to limit the possibilities before you even get started. Sketch, doodle, or cut and paste all the ideas that come to mind no matter how silly or serious. Somewhere in the mix, you will discover an answer to your design quest.

For example, the lovebird portion of the Peruvian hat's graph, shown below (the pattern begins on page 110) was inspired, initially, by traditional Peruvian textiles. This vision was blended with a taller and more detailed bird motif the designer found in another knit garment to create this relatively small, and entirely cute, image.

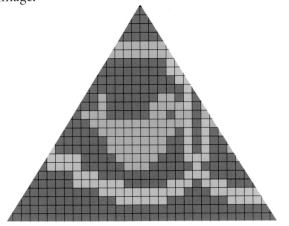

Peruvian Lovebird Hat, page 110

Lay Out the Image

There are several ways to render an image into a useable chart. Lay a piece of knitter's graph paper that has been photocopied onto vellum over your printed image. (Regular knitter's graph paper used over a light table or light source also works.) Shade the squares of the graph paper that outline and fill the printed image. Use a pencil, or several erasable colored pencils—you will want the flexibility of erasable lines when creating your graph.

You can also convert an image into a graph by importing it into photo-manipulation software or knitter's design software. Pixelating an image onscreen will make it more easily transferred to a knitting graph. Pattern design software features the option of importing images onto a graphic background, instantly rendering a useable graph.

Note how the components of the image are distributed across the squares of the graph. Consider the best way to create a curved edge, a delicate line detail, or a subtle color change. A rule of thumb for shaping an image into graph form: If the shape covers more than half of a square, shade it in; less than half, leave it blank. Unfortunately, some details may need to be compromised due to the size and amount of detail that is or isn't possible for your chosen gauge. To effectively graph a design, you must know the gauge and general size of the design before you begin. The size of your original image matters less than the gauge of your finished knitting. However, the graph and image should be proportionally matched. A graph that is ten stitches wide and fifteen rows high will look completely different in fine, fingering-weight socks than it will on a super chunky scarf. You will ultimately save yourself some time and frustration if you do a little basic planning first.

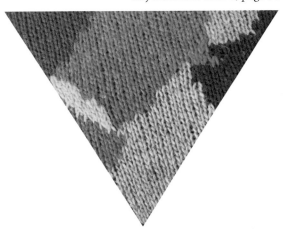

Lily's Bordello Pillow, page 58

Determine Colorwork Techniques

Depending on the grid you created for your graphic piece, you have a few colorwork techniques from which to choose. Are you working with simple geometric shapes, or broad swathes of solid color? The intarsia method will ensure a clean margin between components, and a single-layer fabric will keep the project of lighter weight. More detailed shapes, edges, and components, and multiple patches of color in a wider palette? Fair Isle and stranding techniques allow for more detailed, regular colorwork. Intricate details or occasional bursts of color? Duplicate stitching and other surface embellishments will simplify the knitting process without sacrificing detail.

Consider which colorwork techniques you may be most comfortable working with when making these decisions. The number of colors used in Fair Isle may be limited but simpler to work with, while intarsia has unlimited color options, but can be more tedious to manage.

Knit a Swatch

And now, the fun part: the "test kitchen" of the knitter's world. Knit a sample swatch of your new graphic. If you are aiming to test the viability of the colorwork and not necessarily a particular fabric, you can use stash yarn (in an identical gauge). Consider this a rough draft. How much yarn is being carried across the back? Are the finer details being drowned out by more dominant components? What needs to be adjusted? With the graph in one hand and your knit sample in the other, consider, and then apply, revisions.

Plan a Graphic Project

Taking into consideration the row and stitch count of your graph, desired color palette, and method of colorwork required for execution, plan a knit project featuring your graph. Graphic colorwork is best and most simply applied to stockinette fabric, but options for incorporating textured stitches into your colorwork abound. Anything goes, really. Enjoy the endless array of options that the knitting medium offers, and run with your imagination.

Can You Picture That?

Converting Photos into Graphic Knits

Creating a knitter's graph from a photograph is less complicated that you might think. With a digital photograph of your subject, photo-manipulation software, and a keen eye for detail, a likeness of nearly anyone can be drafted—and incorporated on a garment of choice. (Even without photo-manipulation software, you can create a graphic portrait—it's just slightly more laborious, but far from less rewarding.)

Select your photo. Photographs that feature pockets of light and dark and have key identifying elements are better suited to a simplified graphic motif than photos that are awash with color and fine details. If an image can be distilled to its essential features and still be recognizable (think Warhol's *Mao* and *Marilyn*), then you've found a good candidate for a graphic knit. By default, some details and nuances will be lost or compromised in the photo's conversion to a graph, especially as the gauge increases.

If you plan on working in a photo-manipulation software program to help create your graph, create a digital file (jpeg, preferably) of your chosen photo, either by scanning it, downloading it from the Web, or importing an original from your camera. (If you plan on creating this graph manually, simply print or photocopy the image at the desired size, and proceed to "Transfer your pixelated image to a graph.")

Manipulate your digital file. The key to successful conversion is to tinker with an image's resolution and contrast, striking a balance between pixelation and detail. Experiment with changing the image size, its resolution (dpi), its color balance, contrast, brightness, and other components. Think of each pixel of color as an eventual knit stitch, and you will see both the limitations and the potential of this process. There are no tried-and-true rules at this stage; what you want will vary from project to project.

The graph shown at right was created by pixelating, in Adobe Photoshop, a digital photograph, and then transferring the pixels onto knitter's graph paper.

Calling for three colored yarns on size 7 needles with 5 stitches per inch (2.5 cm) gauge, this hipster portrait is suitable on any wearable or accessory clamoring for the spotlight.

Transfer your pixelated image to a graph. Each pixel on the computer screen is one square; each knit stitch is slightly wider than it is tall. With this ratio in mind, transfer your image to specially proportioned knitter's graph paper (see page 157), or import the image into a software program designed for knitters. The one-pixel to one-stitch transfer will make the portrait seem vertically compressed, unless you account for it by adding an extra row here or there to stretch out the image.

Knit your portrait. Following your graph, work your colorwork magic, and watch your doctored image emerge. Use a duplicate stitch to add bits of color or shadow if the finished piece needs slight adjustment. As mentioned on page 17, it's always advisable to work up a swatch initially, so you don't discover halfway up the torso of your chichi cashmere-blend cowlneck that your homage to Frida Kahlo isn't quite right.

For an iconic silhouetted image, stick with two colors: a main color and one contrasting color (as with the Audrey Hepburn motif, page 135). For a more detailed portrait, you should aim for no more than four or five colors, in order to keep the stranded colorwork at a manageable level, as with the homage to Jon Stewart above.

Crafting a Warhol-inspired portrait may be tempting, but just how many knit Elvises, Marilyns, or Maos do we really need? This graph is an homage to a modern-day icon— Jon Stewart.

Moon Day Yoga Tank, page 120

Where to Begin?

Aside from the obvious sources—knitting books, magazines, and retail stores—there are innumerable places to seek out knitting design and pattern ideas. Please keep fair-use and copyright laws in mind when converting inspiration into a pattern.

Print fabrics ✳ superhero icons ✳ cartoons ✳ brickwork ✳ mosaics✳ fences ✳ flora and fauna ✳ silhouettes ✳ architectural details ✳ city skylines ✳ album covers ✳ botanical drawings ✳ flower shops ✳ T-shirts ✳ wallpaper ✳ logos ✳ signage ✳ typographic details ✳ monograms ✳ stained glass ✳ children's picture books ✳ black-and-white photographs ✳ quilts ✳ cross-stitch patterns (already in graphic form!) ✳ paint chips ✳ wrapping paper ✳ animal prints ✳ paintings ✳ metal work ✳ stencils ✳ woodblock prints ✳ rubber stamps ✳ tile patterns ✳

Blank Slate Projects

Projects that are knit exclusively in stockinette stitch invite the yarns and graphics to take center stage. In these pieces, the colorwork the designer chose for the project is not inextricably linked to the project's structure (unlike, say, the Stripped-Down Petal Rug, page 30 and below). Also, the colorwork of so-called blank slate projects isn't so extensive that substitutions or adjustments would require more precise, all-over doctoring (unlike the Cropped Fair Isle Cardigan, page 68).

Most of the projects in this book are blank slate projects, and are particularly well suited for placing alternate graphs from elsewhere in the book, the Gallery (page 146), or better yet, whipping up your own, and concocting a one-of-a-kind, personalized piece.

Stripped-Down Petal Rug, page 30

Abbreviations

Knitting has its own language. The following is a list of common knitting abbreviations used in the patterns in this book.

beg—begin; beginning; begins

bet—between

BO—bind off; binding off; bound off

CC—contrast color(s)

ch—chain, as in crochet

cm—centimeters

cn—cable needle

CO—cast on; casting on

cont—continue; continuing; continued

dc—double crochet

dec(s)—decrease(s); decreasing; decreased

dpn—double-pointed needle(s)

est—established

foll—follow; following

fwd—forward

g—gram(s)

inc—increase(s); increasing; increased

k—knit

k1-f/b—knit into the front and then the back loop of same stitch

k2tog—knit two stitches together

k3tog—knit three stitches together

kwise—knitwise (as if to knit)

m(s)—marker(s)

MC—main color

mm—millimeter(s)

M1 or **M1-R**—make one stitch (right-slanting increase). Insert the left-hand needle from back to front under the horizontal bar between the stitch on the left-hand needle and the stitch just worked, forming a loop on the left-hand needle; then, with the right-hand needle, knit into the front strand of the loop, thereby twisting the stitch and closing any hole.

M1b—With right-hand needle, pick up loop of stitch one row below next stitch on left-hand needle and place it on left-hand needle; knit into the back of this stitch, slipping it off the needle, then knit into the next stitch.

M1b-r—With right-hand needle, pick up loop of stitch one row below next stitch on left-hand needle and place it on left-hand needle; knit into the front of this stitch, slipping it off the needle, then knit into the next stitch.

M1-L—make one stitch (left-slanting increase). Insert the left-hand needle from front to back under the horizontal bar between the stitch on the left-hand needle and the stitch just worked, forming a loop on the left-hand needle; then, with the right-hand needle, knit into the back strand of the loop, thereby twisting the stitch and closing any hole.

M1-p—make one stitch purlwise. Insert the right-hand needle from back to front under the horizontal bar between the stitch on the left-hand needle and the stitch just worked; place loop on the left-hand needle; then, with the right-hand needle, purl into the front strand of the loop, thereby twisting the stitch and closing any hole.

p—purl

p1-f/b—purl into front and back of same stitch

p2tog—purl two stitches together

patt(s)—pattern(s)

pm—place marker

psso—pass slipped stitch over

pwise—purlwise (as if to purl)

rem—remain; remaining; remainder

rep—repeat(s); repeating; repeated

Rev St st—Reverse Stockinette stitch (purl side of work is used as the right side)

rib—ribbing

rnd(s)—round(s), as in circular knitting

RS—right side

rev sc—reverse single crochet

sc—single crochet

sk—skip

sl—slip

sl st—slip stitch

ssk—slip 2 stitches knitwise, one at a time, from the left needle to the right needle. Insert the left needle tip into the fronts of both slipped stitches and knit them together from this position.

st(s)—stitch(es)

St st—Stockinette stitch

tbl—through the back loop of a stitch

tog—together

wrp-t—wrap and turn

WS—wrong side

wyib—with yarn in back of work

wyif—with yarn in front of work

yf—yarn forward

yo—yarn over

2

Knitting with Stripes

Knitting Stripes is one of the simplest and literally most seamless ways to incorporate colorwork into a knitting project. Loosely defined, a stripe is a block of color that stands apart from the colors on either side. In knitting, this simply means working with one color at a time in a given sequence that may be horizontally, vertically, or diagonally oriented.

A basic horizontal stripe begins with a change in yarn, usually at the beginning of a knit row, and continues uninterrupted to the end. It can be as narrow or wide as you choose with no effect on knitting technique or skill level. Vertical stripes, however, are quite different, as they require the use of either Fair Isle, stranding, or intarsia color knitting techniques depending upon their width. (For extended discussions of intarsia knitting, Fair Isle, stranding, and see chapters 3 and 4, on pages 32 and 66, respectively). For this reason, we will discuss only the basic horizontal knitted stripe in this chapter.

We have included a variety of projects that prove stripes are not the poor cousin of knitted colorwork but rather a dynamic and fun way to introduce color into any project. The Isadora Scarf (page 24) embraces mixing needle sizes, unorthodox unfinished edges and color changes, and is a melée of color. The Bohemian-Chic Yoga Mat Tote (page 26) turns stripes on their sides and ends up with a wraparound diagonal pattern. The Stripped-Down Petal Rug (page 30) extrapolates the generic stripe to its advantage. Through a combination of strategic color changes, short-row shaping, and the substitution of fabric strips for yarn—the key-

Peruvian Lovebird Hat, page 110

Isadora Scarf, page 24

stone element—this project camouflages its stripes and passes as a home decor *tour de force*. Each project uses a combination of even/odd row changes, shaping, texture, and finishing techniques to take stripes to a higher level.

As with any colorwork technique, there are a few logistics that should be considered when working with stripes. If the knit fabric is worked in stockinette stitch, the transition between the main color (MC) and the contrasting color color (CC) will be smooth and uneventful. However, if the knit fabric is worked in garter stitch or a combination of stockinette and garter, the color changes will take on quite a different effect. Changing colors on a purl row will create a line of colorful "bumps" that stand out dramatically. This effect can be used to your advantage, design wise, if tiny doses of color or a pinstripe detail is desired.

Another logistical consideration when working in stripes is how to change colors. If you are working a repeating stripe motif, you can carry the nonworking color yarn loosely up the side of the work as you knit, occasionally wrapping it with the working yarn to prevent it from hanging loosely. The tails may be snipped to a 2" to 3" (5 to 8 cm) length and, as in the Isadora Scarf (page 24), left unwoven as a motley side fringe. Simple striping with an even number of rows per color will allow you to knit and endlessly change colors without the need to break your yarn. Stripes that contain odd numbers of rows will require breaking the yarn

One, Two, Three, Four, Can I Have a Little More?

This book is not meant to be a forum for enumerating all the combinations of rows, yarns, and colorways you can use to your stripe-wielding advantage. (Your options expand exponentially when you consider the options that textured stitches add to your striping potential.) However, here are some design ideas to get you started.

Iconic stripes. Think pirates in tattered broadcloth, mustachioed French men in a Toulouse-Lautrec painting, European soccer scarves, television test patterns. Use tried-and-true striped looks to enhance your designs, with either a nod to or a send-up of tradition.

Don't count, just knit. Let your eyes, not your row counter, be the judge of how best to arrange your stripes. And remember, the most you'll lose by experimenting is time. You can always unravel a creation and reuse the yarn later.

and weaving in all the leftover tails. Ultimately, where and how you stripe is an issue of how many housekeeping duties you want on your to-do list at the end of a project. Every project will have a different set of housekeeping duties; in order to nail down your desired look, you should not shortchange your design based on how many cleanups you'll have at the end.

Isadora Scarf

Whisper-thin mohair in bold stripes will lighten your spirits and put a smile on the face of everyone around you. Wrap this serpentine scarf around and around, or let it dance softly in the breeze. Either way, this lacy, sheer, yet substantial scarf will brighten even the dreariest days of winter.

Designer: Lisa B. Evans

Finished Dimensions
13" × 94½" to 112" (32.5 cm × 2.4 to 2.9 m)

Materials
Yarn
Light-weight mohair/silk blend

Shown: Rowan Kidsilk Haze (70% super kid mohair / 30% silk, 230 yards [210 m] /[25 g]): #583 Blushes, #592 Heavenly, #581 Meadow, #578 Swish, #597 Jelly, #596 Marmalade, #606 Candy Girl, #582 Trance—1 ball each color

Needles
size 13 (9 mm) circular needle, 24" (62.2 cm) long; one size 6 (4 mm) circular needle, 24" (62.2 cm) long

Gauge
18½ sts and 20 rows = 4" (11 cm) in Stockinette stitch (St st)

Always check your gauge! Adjust needle size to obtain correct gauge if necessary.

Notes The entire scarf is worked in Garter st. Refer to the key for stripe sequence and needle size changes only.

When changing colors, break the yarn and weave in the end for 5 to 6 sts.

Scarf

With size 13 (9 mm) circular needle, CO 60 sts. Working back and forth on needles, begin Garter st and stripe sequence from chart, changing to size 6 (4 mm) circular needle as specified in key. Work 6 to 7 full repeats of chart (approximately 94½" to 112" (2.4 to 2.9 m) or to desired length. BO all sts. Trim ends.

KEY

▢	#597 Jelly
▢	#597 Jelly using size 6 (4 mm) needle
▢	#596 Marmalade
▣	#596 Marmalade using size 6 (4 mm) needle
▢	#583 Blushes
▣	#583 Blushes using size 6 (4 mm) needle
▢	#592 Heavenly
▢	#592 Heavenly using size 6 (4 mm) needle
▢	#606 Candy Girl
▣	#606 Candy Girl using size 6 (4 mm) needle
▢	#578 Swish
▢	#578 Swish using size 6 (4 mm) needle
▢	#582 Trance
▣	#582 Trance using size 6 (4 mm) needle
▢	#581 Meadow
▢	#581 Meadow using size 6 (4 mm) needle

Bohemian-Chic Yoga Mat Tote

Yoga and knitting go hand in hand—both are meditative endeavors that don't require a lot of specialized equipment to pursue with success. This mat bag features a clever closure-strap combination that guarantees a snug, cinched pack whether you are standing in *tadasana* while waiting to dash across the street, or gathering your belongings after bidding your instructor *namaste*. The length of the mat bag can be adjusted to the length of your rolled mat, or as desired.

Designer: Anna Kristensen

Finished Dimensions
Before felting: Length: 23" (58.4 cm), diameter 25" (63.5 cm)
After felting: Length 20" (51 cm), diameter 18" (45.7 cm)

Materials
Yarn
Medium, worsted-weight wool/silk blend; medium worsted-weight rayon

Shown: Himalaya Yarn Wool/Silk (60% wool / 40% recycled silk, 80 yards [73.2 m] / 100 g): CH-84 Orange (A) and CH-22 Pink (B), 2 hanks each

Himalaya Yarn Recycled Rayon (100% recycled rayon, 80 yards [73.2 m] / 100 g): multicolor (B), 2 hanks

Needles
One pair size 6 straight needles, 14" (35.6 cm) long; size 6 (4 mm) circular needle, 16" (40.6 cm) long; set of five size 6 double-pointed needles (dpn)

Notions
Tapestry needle; stitch marker; four removable stitch markers

Gauge
16 sts and 24 rows = 4" (10.7 cm) in Garter st, before felting

Always check your gauge! Adjust needle size to obtain correct gauge if necessary.

Notes This pattern uses two types of I-cord: standard I-cord and attached I-cord (see page 145). For the purposes of this pattern only, the standard I-cord will be called "unattached I-cord."

Pattern Stitch
Garter stitch
(any multiple of sts)
Knit every row

Stripe Pattern
✱ Work 4 rows in A, 4 rows in B, 4 rows in C. Repeat from ✱ for stripe pattern.

Body
With A, CO 3 sts. (WS) Begin Garter st and stripe pattern, inc 1 st each edge every RS row, changing colors for stripe pattern every other RS row. Work even until you have 99 sts, ending on a WS row.

Next row (RS): K2tog, knit to last st, k1-f/b. Work even as est, dec 1 st at beg of row and inc 1 st at end of row, every RS row until longest edge of piece measures 21" (53.3 cm) or desired length, ending on a WS row.

Next row (RS): K2tog, knit to last 2 sts, k2tog—97 sts rem. Work even as est, dec 1 st each edge every RS row until 3 sts rem. BO all sts. With A threaded on tapestry needle, sew long edges together. Weave in ends to WS and secure.

Bottom

RS facing, with A and circular needle, pick up and knit 80 sts around one open end of bag; place marker at beginning of rnd. Knit 3 rnds. Change to B.

Bottom Shaping

Dec rnd 1: ✳ K8, k2tog; repeat from ✳ to end of rnd—72 sts rem. Knit 1 rnd.

Dec rnd 2: ✳ K7, k2tog; repeat from ✳ to end of rnd—64 sts rem. Knit 1 rnd.

Dec rnd 3: Change to C. ✳ K6, k2tog; repeat from ✳ to end of rnd—56 sts rem. Knit 1 rnd.

Cont as est in St st and stripe pattern, dec 8 sts every other rnd, working 1 st less before dec in each rnd, until 16 sts rem. End with knit rnd.

Next Rnd: ✳ K2tog; repeat from ✳ to end of rnd—8 sts rem. Cut yarn and thread end through rem sts; pull to tighten. Weave in ends to WS and secure.

Finishing

Top Edge and Loops:
Place four markers evenly distributed along open (top) edge of bag for I-cord loops. With A and double-pointed needles (dpn), CO 3 sts. Begin attached I-cord (see page 145) along top of bag, beginning at side seam.

✳ Work to marker. Change to unattached I-cord (see page 145, I-cord). Work even for 18 rows. Change to attached I-cord, working first st into top edge as close as possible to base of unattached I-cord. Repeat from ✳ 3 times. Work to end. BO all sts. With A threaded on a tapestry needle, sew CO and BO edges together. Weave in ends to WS and secure.

Bottom Edge and Loops:
With A and dpn, CO 3 sts. Work 20 rows of unattached I-cord. Change to attached I-cord, beginning at side seam. Work around entire bottom edge of bag. Change to unattached I-cord. Work even for 20 rows. BO all sts. Fold each unattached I-cord in half and, with yarn threaded on tapestry needle, sew end to bottom edge. Weave in ends to WS and secure.

Side Seam Loops (make 2):
With A and dpn, CO 3 sts. Work 18 rows of unattached I-cord. Bind off all sts. With A threaded on tapestry needle, sew loops along side seam, halfway between top and bottom edges (see illustration). Weave in ends to WS and secure.

Twisted Cord Strap:
Cut one strand (7 yds [6.4 m] long) each of A and B, and two strands of C. Make Twisted Cord (see page 145). Thread cord through one bottom loop, one side seam loop, and all top loops, then back down through other side seam and bottom loops. Tie ends together.

Felt entire bag (see page 43) to your desired dimensions. Dry it in dryer on hot setting.

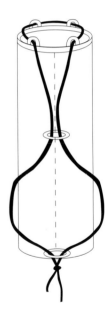

Assembly schematic for yoga mat bag

Stripped-Down Petal Rug

When planning knit projects, don't forget to occasionally think outside the "yarn" box. New or recycled fabric that has been cut into strips can be knit up with gorgeous nuanced results. Select fabrics whose prints or colors harmonize and play off each other. Though not overtly a standard striped design, this rug's ingenious short-row shaping creates a flower-shaped piece that curves in on itself, in flawless, geometric harmony.

Designer: Lisa B. Evans

Finished Dimensions
Approximately 37" (94 cm) diameter at its widest point

Materials
Fabric
1 yard (0.9 m) of fabric in each of twelve colors; 2 yards (1.8 m) of fabric in one contrasting color

Needles
One pair size 13 (9 mm) straight needles, 14" (34.4 cm) long

Notions
P/15 (11.5 mm) crochet hook; jumbo tapestry needle

Gauge
8 sts and 12 rows = 4" (10.7 cm) in Garter st

Always check your gauge! Adjust needle size to obtain correct gauge if necessary.

Notes Petals are worked using short-row shaping.

Petal Pattern

Wrp-t (wrap and turn): Slip 1 st purlwise, yf, pass the slipped st back to your left-hand needle, and then turn the work.

Row 1 (WS): K1, m1, k18, wrp-t.
Row 2 K19, m1, k1—27 sts.
Row 3 K1, m1, k15, wrp-t.
Row 4 K16, m1, k1—29 sts.
Row 5 K1, m1, k12, wrp-t.
Row 6 K13, m1, k1—31 sts.
Row 7 K1, m1, k9, wrp-t.
Row 8 K10, m1, k1—33 sts.
Row 9 K1, m1, k6, wrp-t—34 sts.
Row 10 K8—34 sts.
Row 11 K30, wrp-t.
Row 12 K30.
Row 13 K25, wrp-t.
Row 14 K25.
Row 15 K27, wrp-t.
Row 16 K27.
Row 17 K2tog, k10, wrp-t.
Row 18 K9, k2tog—32 sts rem.
Row 19 K2tog, k14, wrp-t.
Row 20 K13, k2tog—30 sts rem.
Row 21 K2tog, k17, wrp-t.
Row 22 K16, k2tog—28 sts rem.
Row 23 K2tog, k19, wrp-t.
Row 24 K18, k2tog—26 sts rem.
Row 25 K2tog, k24—25 sts rem.
Repeat rows 1 through 25.

Rug

With scissors or a rotary cutter and mat, cut your fabric into 1" (2.5 cm) -wide strips. Begin by folding the fabric accordion-style with the fabric edges extended beyond the folds as shown at right. Cut following the diagram's dashed lines, alternately cutting just shy of the fabric edges on opposite sides.

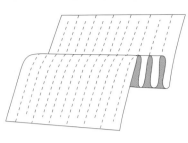

Cutting fabric strips

Using color of your choice, CO 25 sts. Begin petal pattern. Work even until one full repeat of pattern is complete.

✳ Change to new color; k25. Repeat rows 1 through 25 of petal pattern. Repeat from ✳ until 12 petals have been worked. BO all sts.

Finishing

With tapestry needle and last fabric used, sew together CO and BO edges. With crochet hook and contrasting color fabric strips, work single crochet along inside and outside edges of your rug. Trim any uneven fabric edges if desired, or leave them untrimmed for a more rustic appearance.

Optional: Add appliqué leaves or other botanical details to the edge of the rug to further the design.

chapter

3

Intarsia Knitting

Intarsia (pronounced *in-TAHR-jah*) is a versatile style of knitting that allows the knitter to work with many colors at a time, with beautiful results. It can be used to create anything from simple color-block patterns to complex paisley and floral motifs. This technique is an easy method for adding color to any project as it uses only one color at a time and does not carry or strand any others along the back of the work as in Fair Isle knitting. Each color is worked independently and is held to the next by simply wrapping the two strands of yarn around each other at the point of change. Because of this, the finished piece remains a single layer of thickness that isn't bulky from many strands of yarn.

Learning to change colors while keeping the gauge even and without holes is the key to mastering intarsia knitting. A good practice is to start with a simple design such as a vertical stripe, as each section of color is worked independently with separate strands of yarn. When changing from one color to the next, the working yarn is laid to the left side of the work, and the new strand is picked up from underneath, creating a simple, seamless wrap. Continue knitting in the new color, switching to the next color as the pattern requires. Color changes are treated the same whether you are knitting on a right-side/knit row or on a wrong-side/purl row, and always occur on the back of the work so it is unseen on the finished piece. (See Technique Library, page 136, for illustrated instructions on changing colors.)

Lux Pansy Stole, page 34

The Butterfly Effect Cardigan, page 48

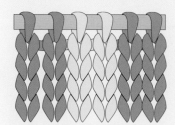

Maintaining the proper gauge while changing colors may seem like an impossible task, particularly if there are many colors in your work. As you knit through the color changes and wraps, you must pay close attention to how tightly the strands are pulled. If the wrap is too loose, a hole will appear. If it is pulled too tightly, the fabric will pucker. A good practice is to check your color changes from the previous row as you work back across them. You can easily adjust the stitches by either giving them a slight tug or by loosening them as you go. Smooth color transitions and an even gauge will become second nature as you continue to work with multiple colors. (See sidebar at right for illustrated examples of correct and incorrect tension.)

Introducing a new color into your work can easily be done by knitting in the new color strand as if it were the working yarn, and then securing the ends. One efficient method of doing so is to lay the loose end across the top of the new working yarn for two or three stitches, and then leave it behind to be trimmed later. The other option for securing the ends is to weave them in with a tapestry needle after the knitting is complete. Waiting until the project is complete isn't the best solution, as holes can develop and possibly damage your work if the ends are left unsecured. Finishing as you go may slow down your knitting a little, but in the long run it will save a lot of time and frustration—not to mention how nice it is to have the tedious job of weaving in ends done when you are!

Tension Samples for Intarsia and Fair Isle

If proper tension is maintained while working intarsia and Fair Isle motifs (as discussed in chapter 4), the transition from one color to the next, no matter how narrow or broad, should be smooth and seamless. Flawed tension will create puckers and gaps at the color margins.

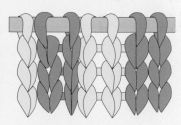

Correct tension creates a smooth transition between color components.

Incorrect tension puckers the fabric between color components, which will become even more pronounced in a felted project.

What could be cozier or more flirtatious than an off-the-shoulder evening wrap? Especially if it is a pink, soft-as-a-cloud merino wool stole with a silky lining. This pansy stole is elegantly styled to drape across your back or over one shoulder, and is big enough to use as a cozy blanket for two! Big, mod pansies make it a great wardrobe accent, but if pansies aren't for you, just change the graphics (using the pansy grid on page 38 as a starting point) and create a statement all your own.

Designer: Lisa B. Evans

Sizes
One size

Finished Dimensions
47³/₄" × 36" (121.3 × 91.4 cm)

Materials
Yarn
Bulky-weight merino wool

Shown: Rowan Big Wool (100% merino wool, 87 yards [79.6 m] / 100 g): #30 Tricky, 5 balls (MC); #20 Lucky, 1 ball (A); #24 Cassis, 3 balls (B)

Needles
One pair size 17 (12.5 mm) straight needles, 14" (35.6 cm) long; size 17 set of five double-pointed needles (dpn)

Notions
Waste yarn; st markers; tapestry needle; 3¹/₂" (8.9 cm) wooden ring or button form; ³/₄" (2 cm) clear button; ¹/₂ yard (45.7 cm) coordinating lining fabric; sewing needle; matching sewing thread

Gauge

8 sts and 12 rows = 4" (10.7 cm) in Stockinette st (St st)

Always check your gauge! Adjust needle size to obtain correct gauge if necessary.

✻

Notes Always knit the first and last sts in a row to create a firm edge that will prevent the edges of the knitting from curling.

Work all color motifs using the intarsia method. Weave in all ends behind a matching color area so strands do not show through the work.

Stole

Using waste yarn and Provisional CO method (see page 39), create chain of 72 sts (approximately 30" [76.2 cm] in length). Using MC and longer needles, pick-up and knit 72 sts along chain. (WS) Begin St st (purl) and row 1 of chart. Work even until chart is complete; place marker (pm) after every 8th st.

Shape End A

Row 1 (RS): Using A, knit to last 16 sts, then place sts on 2 dpns (8 sts on each). Fold last needle to back so WS of last 2 needles are facing each other, then turn work.

Row 2 K2tog, working 1 st from each needle together 8 times, making sure to pull first st tight; purl to end—64 sts rem.

Row 3 Knit to last 16 sts; place sts on 2 dpns. Fold last needle to front so RS of last 2 needles are facing each other. K2tog, working 1 st from each needle together 8 times—56 sts rem.

Row 4 Purl.

Rows 5–12 Repeat rows 1–4—24 sts rem after row 11.

Row 13 Place rem 24 sts on 3 dpns (8 sts on each). Fold last needle to back, then fold first needle to back. All 3 dpns should now be arranged to create an envelope with second dpn to front and working yarn to left. Turn work, p3tog, working 1 st from each needle together 8 times—8 sts rem.

Shape End B

Remove waste yarn from CO edge and place all sts on longer needles, being careful not to twist sts when placing them on needles.

Row 1 (RS): Using A, knit.

Row 2 Purl to last 16 sts, then place sts on 2 dpns (8 sts on each). Fold last needle to front so WS of last 2 needles face each other, then turn work.

Row 3 P2tog, working 1 st from each needle together 8 times, making sure to pull first st tight; knit to end—64 sts rem.

Row 4 Purl to last 16 sts, then place sts on 2 dpns. Fold last needle to back so RS's of last 2 needles face each other. P2tog, working 1 st from each needle together 8 times—56 sts rem.

Row 5 Knit.

Row 6–13 Repeat rows 2–5—24 sts rem after row 12.

Row 14 Place rem 24 sts on 3 dpns (8 sts on each). Fold left needle to back, then fold right needle to back. All 3 dpns should now be arranged to create an envelope with second dpn to front and working yarn to left. Turn work, p3tog, working 1 st from each needle together 8 times—8 sts rem.

Row 15 [K2tog, k1] twice, k1 twice, k1—5 sts rem. Work I-cord for approximately 7" (17.8 cm). Break yarn, leaving 24" (62.2 cm) tail for finishing. Thread through rem sts, pull tight, and fasten off.

KEY

□ St st—knit on RS, purl on WS

□ MC

■ A

□ B

Finishing

Using tapestry needle, MC, and blanket st (see page 143), sew pleats closed along outside edges for approximately 2" to 3" (5.1 to 7.6 cm).

Button: Using dpns and MC, CO 20 sts. Work in St st for 10" (25.4 cm). BO all sts. Wrap knitted piece around wooden ring or button form. Using tapestry needle, MC, and basting or running st, gather piece tight around ring. Stuff excess fabric into covered button to pad and fill in form. Using tapestry needle and MC, attach covered button 1" (2.5 cm) from end A. Using sewing needle and thread, attach clear button to underside of end A. Secure button by sewing through to knitted button on the opposite side.

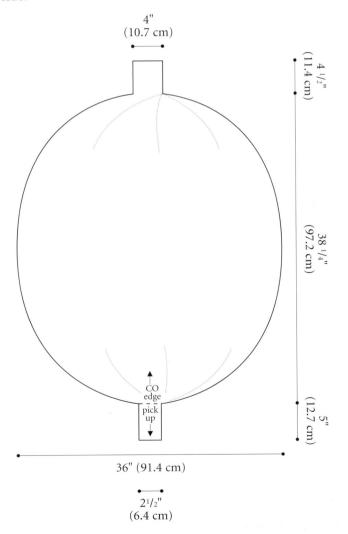

Provisional Cast-on

Provisional casting-on is a technique that allows you to create a piece with matching ends, such as in the Lux Pansy Stole, or any symmetrical project, such as a scarf with decorative ends. The cast-on begins with a long crocheted chain of stitches that serves as a holder to pick up the required number of stitches; it secures the end of your work until you are ready to work the opposite end. At that point, you simply unravel or remove the chain with a few snips of your scissors to expose the live stitches, pick up the stitches with your needle, and begin knitting in the opposite direction.

To create a provisional cast-on, you will need a crochet hook that is larger than the needles you'll be using and about 2 yards (1.8 m) of equal- or larger-gauge waste yarn as that used in your project. Crochet a chain approximately six to ten stitches longer than your knitted piece and fasten the end securely. Leaving a long tail, pick-up the required number of stitches with your project yarn through the bumps on the chain and begin knitting. When you are ready to go in the other direction, undo the end of the chain to allow it to unravel. Carefully pick up the exposed live stitches with your knitting needles, making sure none of them are twisted; if done correctly, the change in direction will be invisible.

I-Cord Loop: Using tapestry needle, attach tail of I-cord to end of side B, forming loop that fits over button. Adjust length of cord as necessary to fit snugly around large button.

Lining: Spread out stole smoothly on large surface with RS down. Lay lining fabric RS up on top of the stole. Fold 3½" to 4" (8.9 to 10.7 cm) of side edges of knitted fabric over onto lining to form facing. Carefully smooth and align fabrics; pin in place. Using sewing needle and thread, baste together knitted piece and fabric. Sew securely; remove pins.

Marimekko-Inspired Felted Needle Case

The fire and ice name is drawn from the color effects of the hand-dyed variegated yarn. Variegated yarn takes Fair Isle knitting a step further in this sweater by creating a design that looks much more complicated than it really is. The chunky weight of the wool will keep even the most resolute hipster chill.

Designer: Lisa B. Evans

Sizes
Small (Medium, Large)
Model shown in size Medium.

Finished Dimensions
Chest: 41 (46, 51)" [104.1 (116.8, 129.5) cm]

Materials
Yarn
Bulky-weight wool/alpaca blend

Shown: Nashua Creative Focus Chunky (75% wool / 25% alpaca, 110 yards [100.6 m] / 100 g): #2380 Oatmeal (MC), 10 balls; # 4899 Khaki Green (B) and #410 Espresso (C), 1 ball each

Nashua Wooly Stripes (100% wool, 88 yards [80.5 m] / 50 g): #WS02 Cognac (A) and #WS07 Spice Market (D), 2 skeins each

Needles
One pair size 9 (5.5 mm) straight needles, 14" (34.4 cm) long; one pair size 10 (6 mm) straight needles, 14" (34.4 cm) long; size 9 (5.5 mm) circular needle, 16" (40 cm) long

Notions
Stitch holders (2); tapestry needle

Gauge

16 sts and 20 rows = 4" (10 cm) in Stockinette st (St st) with larger needles

Always check your gauge! Adjust needle size to obtain correct gauge if necessary.

Pattern Stitches
1 × 3 Rib

(multiple of 4 sts +1)
Row 1 (RS): Slip 1, ✳ p3, k1; rep from ✳ to end of row.
Row 2 Slip 1, ✳ k3, p1; rep from ✳ to end of row.
Rep these rows for pattern.

1 × 3 Rib (for neckband)

(multiple of 4 sts + 1)
Row 1 (RS): K1, ✳ p3, k1; rep from ✳ to end of row.
Row 2 P1, ✳ k3, p1; rep from ✳ to end of row.
Repeat these two rows for the pattern.

✳

Notes When working in Stockinette stitch, slip the first stitch and knit the last stitch of every row.

To maintain a consistent thickness of fabric when working Fair Isle pattern from chart, strand all colors across entire row, even if colors are not indicated on chart over last few stitches.

Back

With MC and size 9 needles, CO 81 (93, 101) sts. Beg 1 × 3 Rib. Work even for 12 rows. (RS) Change to size 10 needles and St st, slipping first st and knitting last st of every row and inc 1 st across first row—82 (92, 102) sts. Work even until piece measures approximately 9" (22.9 cm) from CO edge, ending on a WS row.

(RS) Begin row 1 of chart. Work even until chart is complete, inc 1 st on last row—83 (93, 103) sts. Piece should measure approximately 17" (43.2 cm) from CO edge.

Shape Armholes

(RS) BO 4 (5, 6) sts at beg of next 2 rows—75 (83, 91) sts rem. Work even until armholes measure 8½ (9, 9½)" (21.6 [22.9, 24.1] cm), ending on a WS row.

Shape Shoulders and Neck

(RS) BO 7 (7, 9) sts at beg of next 2 rows, then 6 (8, 9) sts at beg of next 4 rows—37 sts rem. Place rem sts on holder for neckband.

Front

Work as for back until armholes measure 3" (7.6 cm), ending on a WS row.

Shape Neckline

(RS) Work 38 (41, 44) sts, attach second skein, knit center st, place on holder for neckband, knit to end.

Use separate skeins of yarn and work both sides of neckline at same time. Work even for 1 row. Dec 1 st at each neckline edge every RS row 18 times—20 (23, 26) sts remain for each shoulder. Work even until armholes measure 9" (22.9 cm). Shape shoulders and neck as for back.

Sleeves (make two)

With MC and size 9 needles, CO 37 sts. Beg 1 × 3 Rib. Work even for 6 rows. (RS) Change to size 10 needles and St st, slipping first st and knitting last st of every row, inc 1 st each edge this row, every 4 rows 6 (11, 16) times, then every 6 rows 9 (6, 3) times—69 (73, 77) sts.

Work even until sleeve measures 18½ (19, 19½)" (47 [48.3, 49.5] cm), or desired length from CO edge. BO all sts.

Finishing

Block all pieces to measurements. Sew shoulder seams. Set in sleeves. Sew side and sleeve seams. Weave in all ends to WS and secure.

Neckband: With RS facing, using MC, and circular needle, 16" (40 cm) long, beg at right shoulder seam, knit 37 sts from back neck holder, 28 sts evenly down left front neckline—65 sts.

Turn work; purl to end, pick up and purl 27 sts evenly down right front neckline, purl center st from holder—93 sts. Beg 1×3 Rib for neckband. Work even for 7 rows. BO all sts knitwise. Sew right edge of neckband along edge of neckline on RS.

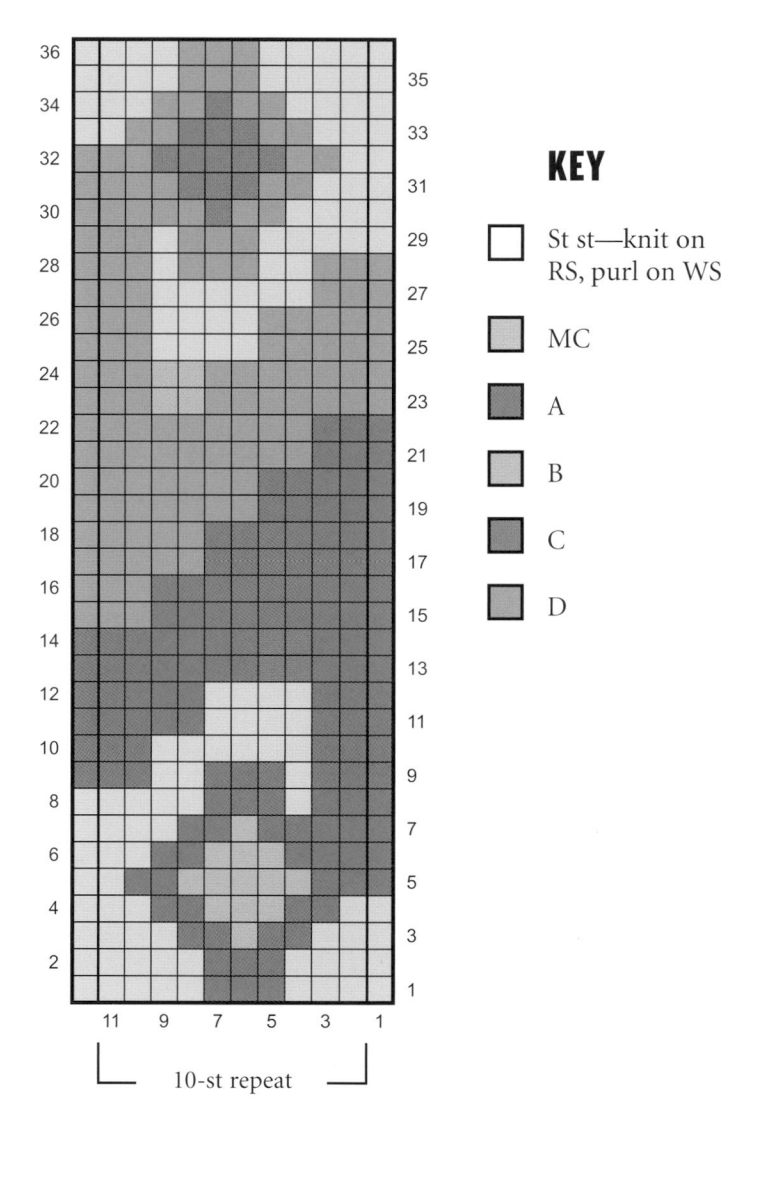

KEY

□ St st—knit on RS, purl on WS

▨ MC

■ A

▥ B

▨ C

▨ D

10-st repeat

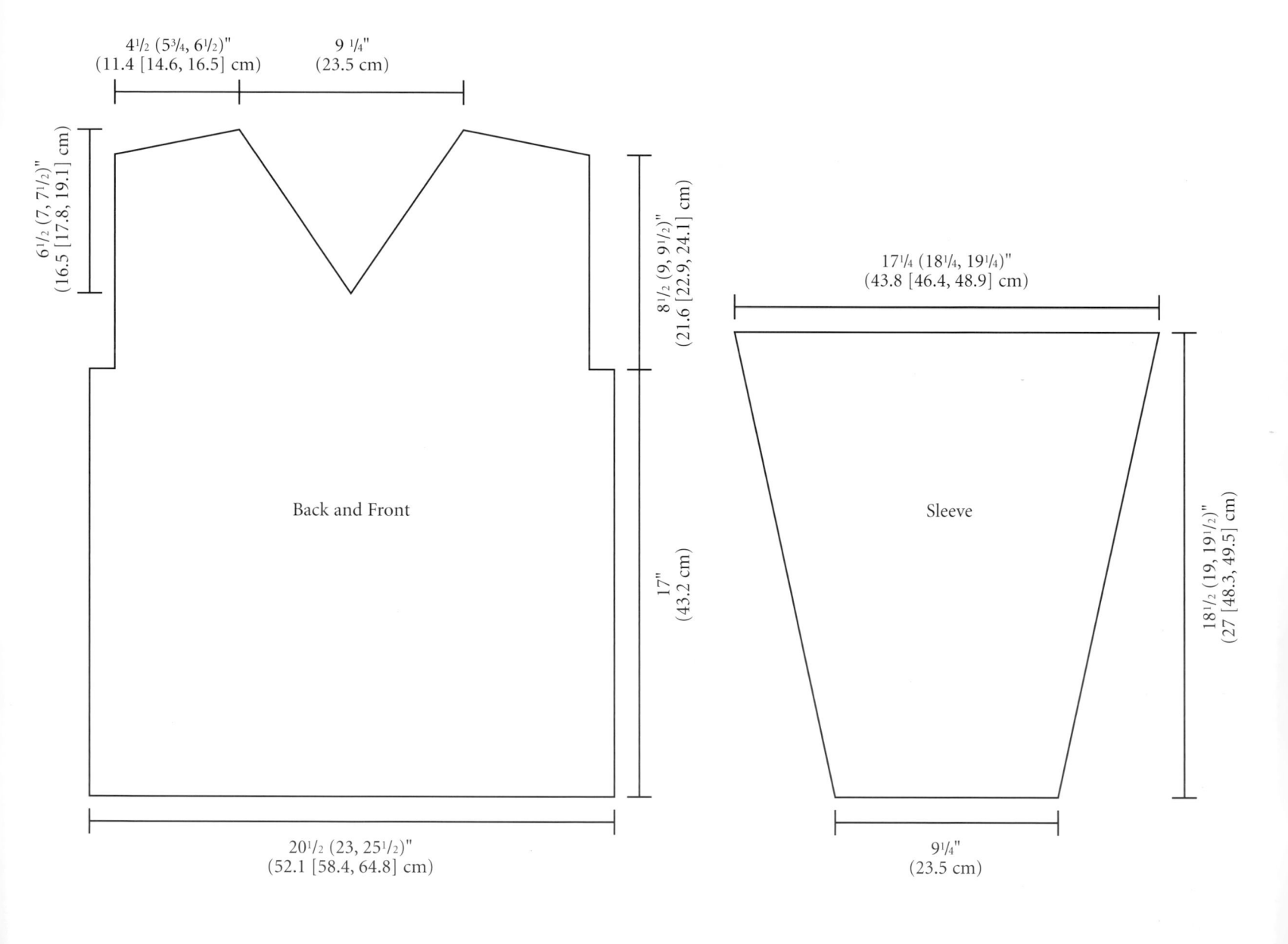

4¹⁄₂ (5³⁄₄, 6¹⁄₂)"
(11.4 [14.6, 16.5] cm)

9 ¹⁄₄"
(23.5 cm)

6¹⁄₂ (7, 7¹⁄₂)"
(16.5 [17.8, 19.1] cm)

8¹⁄₂ (9, 9¹⁄₂)"
(21.6 [22.9, 24.1] cm)

17"
(43.2 cm)

Back and Front

20¹⁄₂ (23, 25¹⁄₂)"
(52.1 [58.4, 64.8] cm)

17¹⁄₄ (18¹⁄₄, 19¹⁄₄)"
(43.8 [46.4, 48.9] cm)

18¹⁄₂ (19, 19¹⁄₂)"
(27 [48.3, 49.5] cm)

Sleeve

9¹⁄₄"
(23.5 cm)

Peruvian Lovebird Hat

Doubled, extra-fine merino wool creates a soft, lofty fabric you'll be loath to put away come spring. Combining jewel-toned rayon-silk yarns on a dark background spins a colorway that rivals stained glass. If you'd like a simpler look, omit the flaps and tassels, and choose a more subdued, complementary palette. (Why would you, though?)

Designer: Rochelle Bourgault

Finished Dimensions

Circumference: 24" (61 cm)
Height: 8½" (21.6 cm)

Materials

Yarn

DK-weight merino wool; light-weight rayon; light-weight rayon/cotton blend

Shown: Jaeger Extra Fine Merino DK (100% extra fine merino wool, 136 yards [124.4 m] / 50 g): #944 Elderberry (MC), 3 balls

Himalaya Yarn 4-Ply Rayon (100% rayon, 80 yards (73.2 m) / 100 g): #RP-155 Copper (A), #RP-166 Leaf (B), #RP-47 Berry (C), 1 skein each

Twisted Sisters Mirage (52% rayon, 48% cotton, 140 yards [128 m] / 50 g): Indigo (D), 1 hank

Needles

Five size 10½ (6.5 mm) double-pointed needles

Notions

M/N-13 (9 mm) crochet hook for finishing; stitch markers; tapestry needle

Gauge

17 sts and 21 rows = 4" (10 cm) in Stockinette st (St st)

Always check your gauge! Adjust needle size to obtain correct gauge if necessary.

Pattern Stitch

2 × 2 Rib

(multiple of 4 sts)

All Rnds: k K2, p2; rep from k to end of rnd

Notes The hat is worked in 2 strands of MC; the chart is worked with a single strand for A, B, and C, and 2 strands for D.

The ear flaps are picked up on the WS of the hat, on the first row above the ribbing.

Hat

With 2 two strands of MC, CO 96 sts. Divide sts onto 4 needles (24 sts each). Join work into a circle, being careful not to twist sts. Place marker (pm) at beg of rnd. Begin 2 × 2 rib. Work even for 4 rnds. Change to St st and work even for 6 rnds. Beg rnd 1 from chart. Work even until entire chart is complete.

Shaping

Continuing in MC, shape hat as follows:

Rnd 1: ✳ K2tog, k14; rep from ✳ to end of rnd—90 sts rem. Work 1 rnd even.

Rnds 2, 4, and 6: Knit

Rnd 3: ✳ K2tog, k13; rep from ✳ to end of rnd—84 sts rem. Work 1 rnd even.

Rnd 5: ✳ K2tog, k12; rep from ✳ to end of rnd—76 sts rem. Work 1 rnd even.

Rnd 7: ✳ K2tog, k8, ssk; rep from ✳ to end of rnd—64 sts rem.

Rnds 8–10: ✳ K2tog; rep from ✳ to end of rnd—8 sts rem.

Cut yarn, leaving 12" (30.9 cm) tail. Thread tapestry needle with tail and weave through rem sts, pulling to close loosely, leaving approximately ¼" to ½" (.6 cm to 1.25 cm) open for braided tassel.

Ear Flaps

WS facing, with 2 strands of MC, beg working even with St #30 of chart on first purl row after ribbing; pick up and knit 14 sts.

Rows 1, 3, 5, 7, and 9 P1, knit to end.
Rows 2, 4, 6, 8, and 10 Purl.
Row 11, 13, 15, and 17 P1, k2tog, knit to end.
Rows 12, 14, 16, and 18 P1, p2tog, purl to end—6 sts rem.
BO all stitches.

Repeat on opposite side of hat, beg even with St #79 of chart.

Finishing

Weave in ends to WS and secure.

Braided Tassels (for top of hat):
Cut six 24" (61 cm) lengths of contrasting colors of your choice. Gather yarn and fold it in half. Using crochet hook, pull folded end of yarn to WS through one st on last row of top of hat.

Pull end back through center opening to RS; thread loose ends through loop and pull tight. Divide 12 strands of yarn into 3 equal sections and braid yarn until tassel is 5" (12.7 cm) long or desired length. Knot yarn at base of braid and trim ends to 3" (7.6 cm) long.

Ear Flaps:
Cut twenty-four 48" (121.9 cm) lengths of contrasting colors of your choice. Divide yarn into 6 sections of 4 strands each. Gather each section of yarn and fold it in half.

Using crochet hook, pull folded end of one section through corner of bottom edge of ear flap; thread loose ends through loop and pull tight. Repeat for opposite corner, then center of ear flap. Braid sections of yarn until tassel is 10" (25.4 cm) long, or

desired length. Knot yarn at base of braid and trim ends to 3" (7.6 cm) long. These braids can be functional—to tie beneath the chin for added warmth—or simply decorative and vaguely Viking-like.

Embroidery:
With single 36" (91.4 cm) strand of D threaded on tapestry needle, embroider floral details on front of hat following diagram. (See pages 139 for a guide to basic embroidery stitches.)

KEY

☐	St st— knit
◼	MC—2 strands
◼	A—1 strand
◼	B—1 strand
◼	C—1 strand
◼	D—1 strand

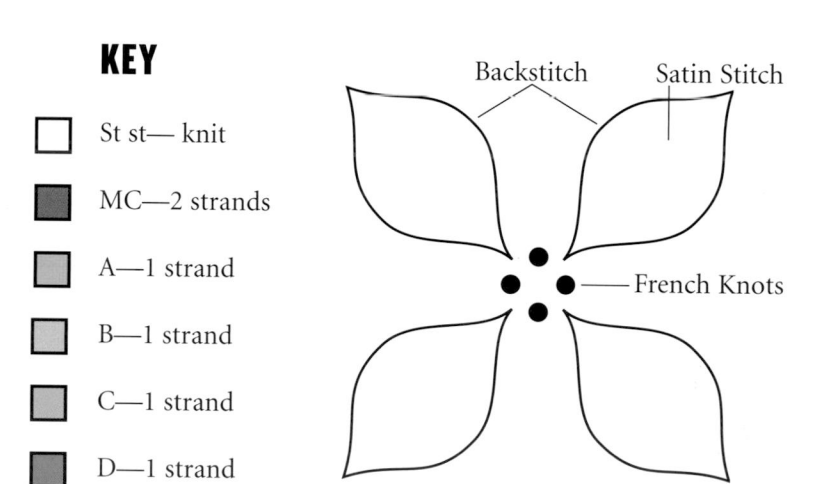

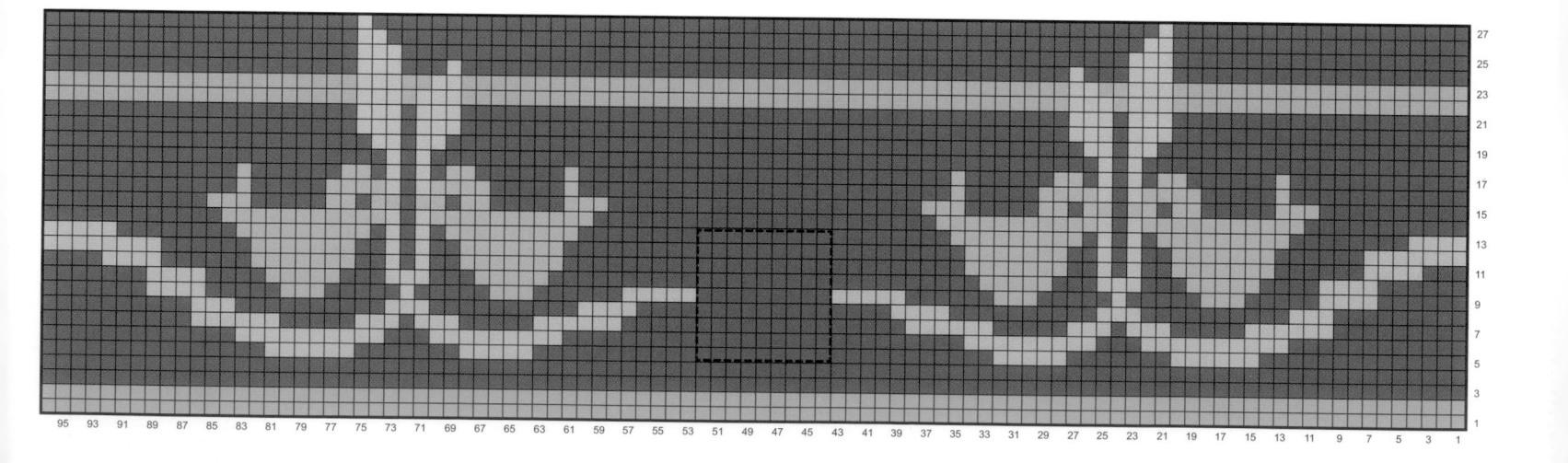

Baby, What's Your Zodiac Socks

Baby What's Your Sign?

Subtly advertise your sun sign—or put out a want ad for the sign of your ideal mate. Who'd have thought that knit socks could make such a play on the singles scene? Even if you're already part of a perfect pair, commemorate your celestially prudent match by knitting both yours and your mate's symbols.

Designer: Rochelle Bourgault

Size
Model shown in women's size Medium.

Finished Dimensions
Circumference: 7³/₄" (19.7 cm)

Length from back of heel to top of ribbing: 7¹/₂" (19.1 cm)

Length from back of heel to tip of toe: 8³/₄" (22.2 cm)

Materials
Yarn
Light-weight wool/cotton blend

Shown: Rowan Wool Cotton (50% merino wool, 50% cotton, 123 yards [113 m] / 50 g), #910 Gypsy (MC), 3 balls; #952 Hiss (A), 1 ball; #946 Elf (B) and #946 Rich (C), a few yards each (optional)

Needles
One pair size 5 (3.75 mm) straight needles, 14" (34.4 cm) long; five size 5 double-pointed needles

Notions
Stitch markers; stitch holders; tapestry needle

Gauge
22¹/₂ sts and 32 rows = 4" (10 cm) in Stockinette st (St st)

Always check your gauge! Adjust needle size to obtain correct gauge if necessary.

Pattern Stitch
1 × 1 Rib
(multiple of 2 sts)
All Rows: ✳ K1, p1; rep from ✳ to end of row

Heel Stripe Pattern (optional)
2 rows MC, 2 rows C, 2 rows B, 1 row MC, 1 row A, 2 rows C, 2 rows A, 1 row B, 1 row MC, 2 rows C, 2 rows A, 2 rows C, 2 rows MC

Notes These socks are knit from cuff to toe. The cuff and ankle portions of the sock are knit in a flat piece in order to accommodate the colorwork, since intarsia cannot be cleanly worked in the round. When colorwork has been completed, the double-pointed needles will be introduced, the stitches redistributed, and the remainder of the sock will be knit in the round. The sock's seam will run up the back of the ankle.

If you choose to substitute your own scrap yarn for working the contrasting colors at the heel, keep in mind that this portion of the sock should be able to fit into a shoe, so even if it's a roomy clog, go easy on the slubby or furry yarns.

The zodiac graphs provided on page 117, 146, and 147 appear upside down, as the socks are knit from top to bottom. If you would like to incorporate them into a project that is knit bottom to top, simply flip them right-side up.

Heel Flap

Place last 22 sts worked (from needles 2 and 3) onto holder for instep. Transfer rem 22 sts onto 1 needle (beg of rnd marker will be in center of these sts). Working heel stripe pattern as shown (optional), or continuing in MC if desired, work heel as follows:

Row 1 (RS): ✳ Sl 1, k1; rep from ✳ to end of row
Row 2 Sl 1, purl to end of row.
Repeat these two rows 11 times.

Turn Heel

Setup rnd 1: Sl 1, k12, k2tog, k1, turn.

Setup rnd 2: Sl 1, p5, p2tog, p1, turn.

Rnd 3: Sl 1, knit to 1 st before gap (created by p2tog of previous row), k2tog across gap, k1, turn.

Right Sock

With straight needles and MC, CO 44 sts. Beg 1 × 1 rib. Work even for 4 rows, changing colors each row as follows (optional):

C, B, A, C. Change to MC and St st. Work even for 4 rows.

Beg zodiac motif as follows:

K21, place marker (pm), work row 1 from chart across 18 sts, pm, knit to end. (See tip at right for instructions on changing the placement of your symbol, or for working a different symbol.) Work even until entire chart is complete. Transfer sts to 4 dpn (11 sts each), dropping st markers. Join the work into a circle, being careful not to twist sts. Pm at beg of rnd. Beg St st. Work even for 5 rows, ending with third needle on last row.

Tip

Each zodiac motif is 18 sts wide. You may choose to adjust the specific placement of your motif based on where on your ankle you would like it to appear. Simply decide where to start the motif, place a st marker, work to the end of the chart, and place a second marker. The Virgo sample (opposite, left) sets the motif 22 sts in from the back seam; the Aries sample (opposite, right) sets the motif 24 sts in from the back seam. (You could also knit symmetrical motifs—one on each side of the sock—thereby creating identical socks. Why make your life more complicated by needing to choose which sock belongs on which foot?)

Remember, a knit motif can be incorporated into any panel of any project. With these socks, even the soles of the feet are blank canvases suitable for enhancement.

If you'd like your sock to be taller or squatter, for it to feature pattern sts or to have a longer rib, by all means, modify, modify, modify! The gusset, heel, and toe shaping won't change if you tweak the ankle's style. Just keep track of what you do so you can repeat it for the second sock.

Rnd 4: Sl 1, purl to 1 st before gap (created by k2tog of previous row), p2tog across gap, p1, turn.

Rep rnds 3 and 4 three times (all sts should have been worked)—14 sts rem.

Gusset

Using first needle, knit across rem 14 sts, pick up and knit 11 sts along side of heel flap; transfer sts from st holder back onto second and third needles (11 sts each).

Knit across second and third needles; with fourth needle, pick up and knit 11 sts along other side of heel flap. Knit across 7 sts from first needle to beg of rnd—58 sts.

Dec rnd: Using first needle, knit to last 3 sts, k2tog, k1. Knit across second and third needles. Using fourth needle, k1, ssk, knit to end—56 sts rem. Work even for 1 row.

Rep last 2 rnds 6 times—44 sts rem (11 sts each needle).

Foot

Determine desired length of your sock by measuring your foot from the back of your heel to the tip of your longest toe (the model measures 8³/₄" [22.2 cm]). Work even until foot measures 2" (5.1 cm) less than desired length.

Toe

Dec rnd: Using first needle, knit to last 3 sts, k2tog, k1. Using second needle, K1, ssk, knit to end. Using third needle, knit to last 3 sts, k2tog, k1. Using fourth needle, K1, ssk, knit to end—40 sts rem. Work even for 1 rnd.

Rep last 2 rnds 4 times—24 sts rem (6 sts each needle).

Rep dec rnd only 4 times—8 sts rem (2 sts each needle).

Cut yarn, leaving 8" (20.3 cm) tail. Thread tapestry needle with tail and weave through rem sts twice, pulling to close tightly.

Left Sock

Work as for right sock to beg of chart. Beg zodiac motif as follows: K5, pm, work row 1 from chart across 18 sts, pm, knit to end.

Complete as for right sock.

Finishing

Weave in ends to WS and secure.

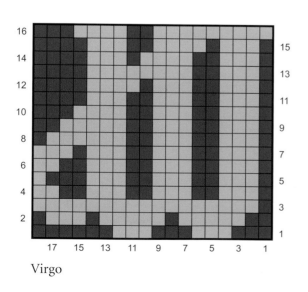

Virgo

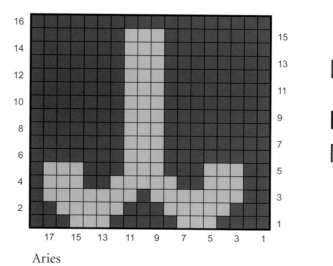

Aries

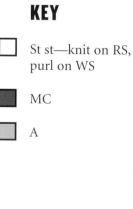

KEY

☐ St st—knit on RS, purl on WS

■ MC

☐ A

chapter

5

Embellishing Your Knitting

Graphic Color Work Using Duplicate Stitch, Embroidery Stitches, and Other Alterations

Graphic knitted colorwork is not strictly confined to projects created from the ground up with needles and yarn. Incorporating color, pattern, and decorative motifs into a knit fabric can be implemented with such everyday craft items as a paintbrush or a tapestry needle. The projects in this chapter employ a variety of techniques, all of which can be applied to any project, garment, or accessory that strikes your fancy.

Duplicate Stitch

One of the most versatile techniques any knitter can learn is the duplicate stitch. It is aptly named because it literally duplicates an existing knit stitch by tracing it. It is an embroidery stitch that is worked onto the knitted fabric with a tapestry needle and yarn, completely covering the stitch underneath and changing its color. It is useful for adding small-scale detail work such as a few dots of color on a floral motif or more elaborate designs that don't lend themselves well to either Fair Isle or intarsia knitting.

Another use for the duplicate stitch is as knitter's Wite-out. It is a perfect tool for correcting small errors in color-

Moon Day Yoga Tank, page 120

Peruvian Lovebird Hat, page 110

work, such as in a fine Fair Isle project. Once you learn the duplicate stitch, you will never have to sweat those slight mistakes again.

The Moon Day Yoga Tank (page 120) relies on duplicate stitch for its highly detailed *om* motif while the Eve's Garden Cover-up Coat (page 98) uses a mix of both Fair Isle and duplicate stitch to create its visually complicated colorwork pattern. Either pattern could effectively be knit in the Fair Isle technique, but it would require long lengths of stranded color behind the knitted work, which could potentially snag or pucker the fabric and cause problems for the wearer. Duplicate stitch allows the fabric to remain more fluid and lighter weight because the second color of yarn is not carried throughout the work. The Audrey Hepburn Embellished Sweater (page 132) uses duplicate stitch to embellish a simple purchased sweater; this decorative technique can be applied to any knitted garment from the store that craves a bit of personalization. This graphic could be knitted via a stranding technique as well. (Duplicate stitch instructions are given on page 143.)

Embroidery Stitches

Any knit garment, whether handmade or store bought, can be enhanced with embroidery stitches. Think of it as the icing on a cupcake: It's not essential, but it can add a certain *je ne sais quoi* to an otherwise plain canvas.

The Mendhi Sleeves (page 128) call for an elegant array of embroidery stitches, using a henna-colored yarn for a design detail that appears to be a hand-painted tattoo. Planning an embroidery pattern such as this on knitter's graph paper is advisable; it's easier to erase rogue sketches than it is to snip out a series of stitches. A freeform, improvised stitched design could be just as suitable for your project; if so, use the embroidery stitches illustrated on pages 139–143 as though they are your palette of paints and dive in. Remember, if it doesn't work the first, second, or *nth* time around, you can always snip the embroidery yarn and try again.

Painting, Dyeing, and Bleaching Knit Fabric

Just like woven fabric, knit fabric can be painted, dyed, and bleached to achieve additional color effects. This technique is used effectively in the Star-Bellied Toddler Sweater (page 124). Planning the design to be dyed or bleached and creating a stencil of it will ensure a design's success. Unlike embroidery, bleaching is permanent and must be done carefully or you may end up with a different design entirely! Instructions for bleaching are given on page 126 with the toddler sweater pattern. For an additional level of detail, embellish the bleach work with embroidery or duplicate stitch. For additional embellishment ideas, see page 131

119

Moon Day Yoga Tank

Yoga is hot, not to mention sweaty, and environmental consciousness is even hotter. Soy-based polypropylene yarn is the perfect choice for a knitter who wants to take care of the world and her body at the same time. This racerback tank not only stretches and bends with each pose, it wicks away the moisture and keeps you cool and dry through *savasana*.

Designer: Lisa B. Evans

Sizes

Small (Medium, Large)
To fit bust 32–34 (36–38, 40–42)" (81–86 [91–96, 101–106] cm)
Model Shown in size small.

Finished Measurements

Chest: 27 (31, 35)" (68.6 [78.7, 88.9] cm)

Materials

Yarn

Medium-weight soy/polypropylene blend

Shown: Knit One, Crochet Too Wick (53% soy / 47% poly propylene, 120 yds (110 m) / 50 g), #464 gold (MC), 4 balls; #533 avocado (CC), 1 ball.

Needles

Size 7 (4.5 mm) circular needle, 24" (61 cm); one pair 14" (34.4 cm) straight needles, same size.

Notions

Stitch markers (in 3 colors); stitch holders; tapestry needle.

Gauge

20 sts and 28 rows = 4" (10 cm) in Stockinette stitch (St st)

Always check your gauge! Adjust needle size to obtain correct gauge if necessary.

Notes The body of the pullover is worked in the round in St st, while the top portion (front, T-back, and straps) are worked back and forth on straight needles.

Body shaping is worked at markers. Because shaping for the front and back occur at different intervals, separate instructions will be given for each. However, shaping for front and back will be worked at the same time, so be sure to follow shaping instructions carefully. You might want to use color-coded stitch markers, which will help greatly as you work the shaping (i.e., one color marker for both left and right fronts, a second color for both left and right backs, and a third color for center back to show beginning of round).

Pattern Stitch
Seed stitch in the round

(odd number of stitches.)
Rnd 1: K1, ✳ p1, k1; rep from k to end of rnd.
Rnd 2: P1, ✳ k1, p1; rep from k to end of rnd.
Repeat these 2 rnds for Seed stitch pattern.

Body

With circular needle and MC, CO 147 (167, 187) sts. Join work into a circle, being careful not to twist sts. Place marker (pm) at beg of rnd. Beg Seed st. Work even for 5 rnds. Change to St st and work even for 11 rnds, place markers after the following sts on the last rnd: #14 (15, 16) (left back), #61 (66, 71) (left front), #86 (101, 116) (right front), 133 (152, 171) (right back).

Shape Body
Front Shaping

Note: Remember to work front and back shaping simultaneously.

Dec Rnd 1: Work to 2 sts before second marker, k2tog, work to third marker, ssk, work to end, slip end of rnd marker. Rep Dec Rnd 1 every 4 rnds 8 times.

Back Shaping

Dec Rnd 2: Work to first marker, ssk, work to 2 sts before fourth marker, k2tog, work to end, slip end of rnd marker.

Rep Dec Rnd 2 every 5 rows 7 times—113 (133, 153) sts rem after all decs are complete.

Work even until piece measures 10 (10½, 11)" (25.4 [26.7, 27.9] cm) or desired length from beg.

Front Shaping

Note: Remember to work front and back shaping simultaneously.

Inc Rnd 1: Work to 1 st before second marker, m1b, work to third marker, m1b-r, work to end, slip end of rnd marker.

Rep Inc Rnd 1 every 3 rnds 7 times.

Back Shaping

Inc Rnd 2: Work to first marker, m1b-r, work to 1 st before fourth marker, m1b, work to end, slip end of rnd marker.

Rep Inc Rnd 2 every 7 rnds twice—135 (155, 175) sts after all incs are complete.

Break yarn.

Shape Armholes

Slip last 16 (17, 18) and first 17 (18, 19) sts of rnd to holder for back, removing markers—102 (120, 138) sts rem. (RS) Rejoin yarn and change to straight needles, removing markers. Working back and forth on rem sts, BO 8 (12, 16) sts at beg of next 2 rows, 3 sts at beg of next 4 rows, then 2 sts at beg of next 4 rows. Dec 1 st every other row 3 times, then every 4 rows once, as follows: Ssk, work to last 2 sts, k2tog—58 (68, 78) sts rem.

Shape Neckline

(RS) Work 24 sts, attach second ball of MC, BO center 10 (20, 30) sts, work to end. Use separate balls of MC and work both sides of neckline at same time. Dec 1 st each side every 4 rows twice, then every 6 rows twice, and AT THE SAME TIME, BO 4 sts each neck edge twice, 2 sts twice, then dec 1 st each neck edge every other row once, every 4 rows once, then every 6 rows once, as follows: At left neck edge, work k2tog; at right neck edge, work ssk—4 sts rem. Work even for 2" (5.1 cm), ending on WS. Place sts on holder.

Shape T-Back

RS facing, rejoin yarn to sts on holder and change to straight needles. BO 3 sts, work to end. BO 2 sts at beg of next 5 rows. Dec 1 st each side every other row twice, then every 4 rows once, as follows: Ssk, work to last 2 sts, k2tog—14 (16, 18) sts rem. Work even for 8 (10, 12) rows. Inc 1 st each side every 4 rows 3 times, as follows: K1, m1b-r, work to last st, m1b, k1—20 (22, 24) sts. Work even for 1 row.

Shape Neck

(RS) Work 8 sts, attach second ball of MC, BO center 8 (10, 12) sts, work to end. Use separate balls of MC and work both sides of neckline at same time. Inc 1 st on second RS row, then every 4 rows twice and, AT THE SAME TIME, BO 2 sts each neck edge once, dec 1 st each neck edge every other row twice, then every 4 rows 3 times, as follows: At left neck edge, work k2tog; at right neck edge, work ssk—4 sts rem. Work even until straps measure same as for front, ending on WS.

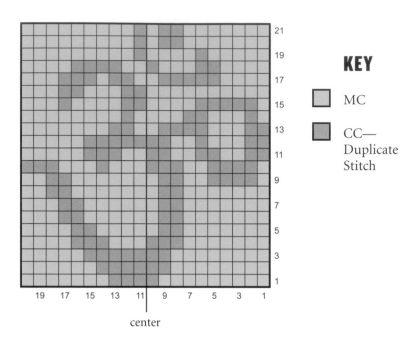

KEY

☐ MC

■ CC—
Duplicate
Stitch

center

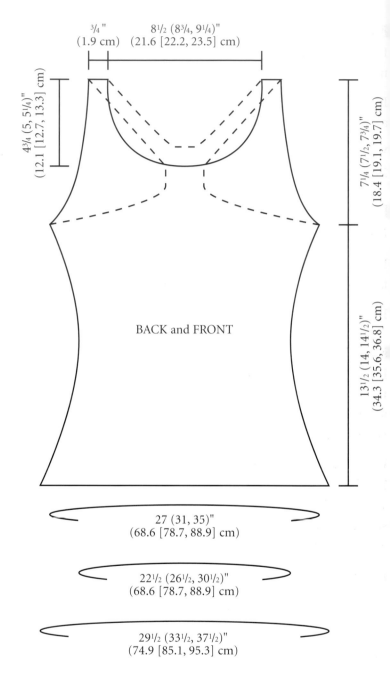

¾" (1.9 cm)

8½ (8¾, 9¼)" (21.6 [22.2, 23.5] cm)

4¾ (5, 5¼)" (12.1 [12.7, 13.3] cm)

7¼ (7½, 7¾)" (18.4 [19.1, 19.7] cm)

BACK and FRONT

13½ (14, 14½)" (34.3 [35.6, 36.8] cm)

27 (31, 35)" (68.6 [78.7, 88.9] cm)

22½ (26½, 30½)" (68.6 [78.7, 88.9] cm)

29½ (33½, 37½)" (74.9 [85.1, 95.3] cm)

Finishing

Straps: Adjust length of front and back straps if necessary, so they fit with a slight stretch. With MC, graft or sew left front strap to left back strap. Repeat for right straps.

Neck Edging: With crochet hook and MC, work single crochet edging around neck and armholes.

Duplicate Stitch Motifs: Beg at center back, on first row of body decs, pm for motifs after the following sts: #2 (4, 5), #26 (31, 36), #50 (58, 66), #74 (85, 97), #98 (112, 127), #122 (139, 158). With tapestry needle and CC, work 6 separate motifs from chart in Duplicate Stitch (see page 143), beg each motif at a st marker. For the center front motif, first count up 17 rows from the first row of body decs. Then find the center point between the two front shaping lines, and count back 10 sts to the right. Beg center front motif at this point. The center line in the chart should line up with the center point between the two front shaping lines.

Weave in ends to WS and secure.

Star-Bellied Toddler Sweater

This simply shaped roll-neck sweater can be a wardrobe staple for any hip kid (who has an even hipper knitter in his or her life). Note the variety of effects bleaching creates when working with other colors (see page 126). Always knit—and bleach—a sample swatch before implementing this embellishment technique.

Designer: Stewart Watkins

Sizes

Small (Medium, Large)
To fit 3–6 (9–12, 18–24) months
Model shown in 3–6 months (Small).

Finished Dimensions

Chest: 20 (23½, 28) " (50.8 [59.7, 71.1] cm)

Materials
Yarn

Light-weight cotton

Shown: Halcyon Yarns Casco Bay Cotton Worsted (100% cotton, 135 yards (123.4 m) / 3.4 oz [97.2 g]): #103 Black, 3 (4, 4) mini-cones. (Also shown in #205 Green, #122 Blue, and #135 Red.)

Needles

One pair size 5 (3.75 mm) straight needles, 14" (34.4 cm) long; one pair size 7 (4.5 mm) straight needles, 14" (34.4 cm) long; size 5 circular needle, 12" (30.5 cm) long, for neckline

Note: you may use a set of 4 or 5 double-pointed needles instead of a circular needle.

Notions

Stitch markers; stitch holders; tapestry needle; bleaching templates (page 127), printed on cardstock; craft knife; ruler; masking tape; 1 piece of cardboard larger than template; bleach pen

Gauge

18 sts and 32½ rows = 4" (10 cm) in Stockinette st (St st) with size 7 (4.5 mm) needles

Always check your gauge! Adjust needle size to obtain correct gauge if necessary.

Back

With size 5 straight needles, CO 45 (53, 63) sts. Beg St st. Work even until piece measures 2" (5.1 cm) from CO edge. Change to size 7 needles. Work even until piece measures 12 (14, 16)" (30.5 [35.6, 40.6] cm) from CO edge, unrolled, ending on a WS row.

Neckline Shaping

Divide sts for neckline as follows:

BO 12 (15, 18) sts, k21 (23, 27) sts and place on holder for back neck, work to end. BO rem 12 (15, 18) sts.

Front

Work as for back until piece measures 9.5 (11.5, 13.5)" (24.1 [29.2, 34.3] cm) from CO edge, unrolled, ending on WS row.

Neckline Shaping

Divide sts for neckline as follows:

K16 (19, 22) sts, place center 13 (15, 19) sts on holder for front neck, attach second mini-cone, knit to end of row. Use separate mini-cones of yarn and work both sides of neckline at the same time. Work even for 1 row. Dec 1 st at each neckline edge every

RS row 4 times—12 (15, 18) sts rem for each shoulder. Work even until front measures same as back. BO shoulder sts.

Sleeves (make two)

With size 5 needles, CO 23 (25, 29) sts. Beg St st. Work even until the piece measures 1¹/₂" (3.8 cm) from CO edge, ending on WS row. Change to size 7 needles. Inc 1 st each edge every other row 5 (6, 6) times, then every 4 rows 6 (7, 9) times—45 (51, 59) sts. Work even until sleeve measures 7¹/₂ (9¹/₂, 11)" (19.1 [24.1, 27.9] cm) from CO edge, unrolled. BO all sts.

Finishing

Sew shoulder seams. Mark 5 (5³/₄, 6¹/₂)" (12.7 [14.6, 16.5] cm) down from each shoulder along each arm-hole edge. Sew in sleeves between markers. Sew side and sleeve seams.

Neckband: RS facing, using circular needle, beg at left shoulder seam, pick up and knit 12 sts to front holder. Work across 13 (15, 19) sts from front neck holder, pick up and knit 12 sts to right shoulder, and knit across 21 (23, 27) sts from back neck holder—58 (62, 70) sts.

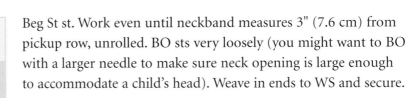

Beg St st. Work even until neckband measures 3" (7.6 cm) from pickup row, unrolled. BO sts very loosely (you might want to BO with a larger needle to make sure neck opening is large enough to accommodate a child's head). Weave in ends to WS and secure.

Bleaching: Enlarge template of your choice (opposite), or draw desired shape onto cardstock or other durable paper. Using craft blade, carefully cut out center of shape, employing ruler as needed for straight edges.

Design Variation

✳ Create the four-leaf clover with intarsia instead of bleach, and outline the shape with a running stitch in a contrasting color. Incorporate a simple Fair Isle band along the bottom edge. Choose six or seven yarns from your stash (that are of equal gauge, of course) and knit it up in randomly sized, vibrant stripes. Options abound!

Center stencil and tape it to front of sweater using tape rolls on back of template, just inside open edge. Place cardboard between front and back of sweater. With wider end of bleach pen, coat sweater in area of opening of stencil. Let piece sit overnight. Rinse away bleach with cold water. Stuff sweater with paper towels until it is dry.

Note: If you are using yarn other than what is called for, or in colors not shown here, it is recommended that you do a test swatch in order to determine the finished color of the bleached area.

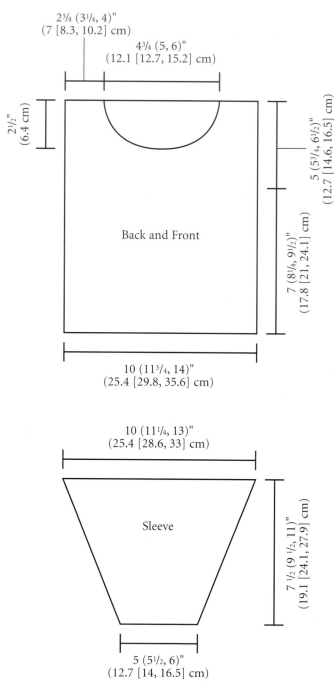

2³⁄₄ (3¹⁄₄, 4)"
(7 [8.3, 10.2] cm)

4³⁄₄ (5, 6)"
(12.1 [12.7, 15.2] cm)

2¹⁄₂"
(6.4 cm)

5 (5³⁄₄, 6¹⁄₂)"
(12.7 [14.6, 16.5] cm)

Back and Front

7 (8¹⁄₄, 9¹⁄₂)"
(17.8 [21, 24.1] cm)

10 (11³⁄₄, 14)"
(25.4 [29.8, 35.6] cm)

10 (11¹⁄₄, 13)"
(25.4 [28.6, 33] cm)

Sleeve

7 ¹⁄₂ (9 ¹⁄₂, 11)"
(19.1 [24.1, 27.9] cm)

5 (5¹⁄₂, 6)"
(12.7 [14, 16.5] cm)

* Photocopy templates at 325% for model shown.

Mendhi Sleeves and Collar

Send a secret message to someone special with this take on the traditional Middle Eastern henna body decoration. These lacy accessories are so quick and easy to knit you can make a pair for every outfit or mood. Express yourself freely with a needle and thread, no commitment necessary.

Designer: Lisa B. Evans

Finished Dimensions

Sleeves: 7" x 11½" (17.8 x 29.2 cm)
Collar: 2¾" x 10½" (7.0 x 26.7 cm)

Materials
Yarn

Medium, aran-weight wool/mohair blend

Shown: Rowan Kid Classic (70% lambswool / 26% kid mohair / 4% nylon, 151 yards [138.1 m] / 50 g): #841 Lavender Ice (A), 2 balls

Rowan Kidsilk Haze (70% super kid mohair / 30% silk, 227 yards [207.6 m] / 25 g): #584 Villain (B), 1 ball

Needles

One pair size 8 (5 mm) straight needles, 14" (34.4 cm) long

Notions

H-8 (5 mm) crochet hook (optional), tapestry needle, twenty ¼" (6 mm) buttons

Gauge

18 sts and 24 rows = 4" (10 cm) in Stockinette st (St st) with A

Always check your gauge! Adjust needle size to obtain correct gauge if necessary.

Pattern Stitch
Honeycomb Lace for Collar

(panel of 12 sts)
Row 1 (RS): K2, [yo, k2tog] 4 times, k2.
Row 2 Purl.

Row 3 K2, [k2tog, yo] 4 times, k2.
Row 4 Purl.
Repeat these 4 rows for pattern.

Notes Sleeves and collar are knit in a honeycomb lace pattern with a combination of yarnovers and decreases. Check the stitch count periodically after completing a row as it is easy to drop stitches without noticing.

Sleeves (make two)

With A, CO 27 sts. Beg row 1 of chart. Work even until entire chart is complete, working decs as indicated in chart—1 st rem.

Fasten off, but do not cut yarn. Work slip-knot chain or crochet chain long enough to comfortably reach to and wrap around your middle finger like a ring, then back to end of sleeve. Fasten off, leaving 6" (15.2 cm) tail. Thread tapestry needle with tail, and securely attach end of chain to beg of chain.

Finishing

Weave in ends to WS and secure. Sew 8 buttons evenly spaced along one edge of sleeve, beg ¼" (6 mm) up from CO edge and end ¼" (6 mm) before beg of shaping. Sleeves should fit snugly.

Embroidery Details: With tapestry needle and B, work embroidery from diagram or create your own, using as many different types of sts as you like. Let your imagination go!

Collar: CO 12 sts. Knit 2 rows. Beg honeycomb lace for collar. Work even until collar is desired length and fits, stretching slightly. BO all sts.

Weave in ends to WS and secure. Sew 4 buttons evenly spaced along one end of collar, placing 1 button in each corner.

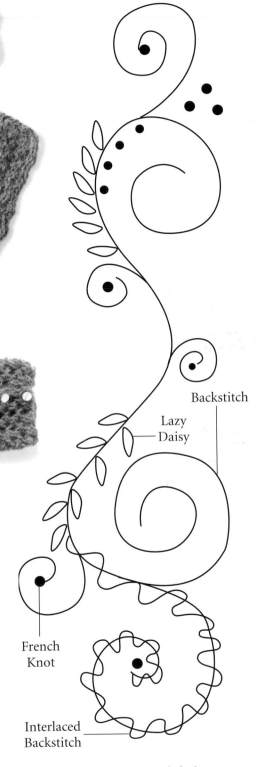

Backstitch

Lazy
Daisy

French
Knot

Interlaced
Backstitch

Embroidery template, left sleeve
Note: Reverse template for right sleeve

Clearinghouse of Embellishment Ideas

The following is an array of embellishment ideas for any hand-knit or purchased garment, item, or accessory. Directions for all of these methods are not included in this book, though a few are included in some project instructions and in the Embellishment Library, page 139. With the tips and techniques illustrated throughout this book, however, we hope that you will be inspired to use your own design vision to create unique projects.

Appliqué to your heart's content. Knit flowers, leaves, braids, cords, or any other shapes you and your needles can come up with, and anchor them to your finished piece with a needle and thread.

Weave. Incorporate a series of eyelets or slipped stitches and weave yarns, fabric strips, ribbons, or trim through the holes. More a decorative than a knit embellishment, this still uses the principles of color play.

Unravel. Drop stitches from your needles, snip strategically, or cut a fringe—unraveling a portion of your knit item adds texture with a touch of danger (just how much will unravel?).

Tricoterie avec frontiers (*knitting with borders*). Pick up stitches along a finished edge and create a border detail in a yarn or fiber of your choice. The edging can be as simple as a single crochet or as elaborate as an Aran braid.

Picking up where you left off. Pick up stitches in the middle of a project to add a patch, a pocket, a doodad, or a whimsical detail of choice, that incorporates beads, charms, or other ornaments. Like graphic knits themselves, embellishment ideas come from anywhere and everywhere. Keep your eyes peeled, your sketchbook or journal open, and your knitter's stash well stocked.

KEY

☐ St st—knit on RS, purl on WS

⊡ Purl on RS, knit on WS

⊙ Yo

⊠ K3tog

⊠ or ⊠ K2tog

⊠ P2tog

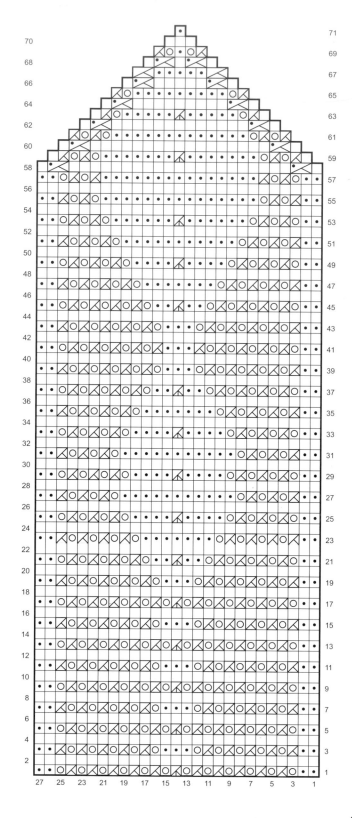

Audrey Hepburn
Embellished Sweater

This duplicate-stitched, purchased sweater is one part Eliza Doolittle, in its transformation from ho-hum to glam, and one part Holly Golightly, in its classic styling and sassy motif. Either way you look at it, it's 100 percent Audrey. If you'd like to use this graph in an original project, exchange the duplicate stitch for stranding, and incorporate it into a sweater or accessory pattern knit "from scratch."

Designer: Rochelle Bourgault

The directions provided are intended to be general enough to apply to any duplicate stitch embellishment project. We have listed materials specific to this project, though it is likely that nearly every project will vary.

Materials
Purchased sweater in style and size of your choice (shown: light pink boatneck cowl sweater, women's XS)

Yarn
Light-weight cotton

Shown: Rowan Cotton Glacé (100% cotton, 125 yards [114.3 m] / 50g): #816 Mocha Choc, 1 ball

Notions
Waste yarn or masking tape for outlining duplicate st area; tapestry needle; embroidery hoop (optional)

Gauge
Purchased sweater: 24 sts and 40 rows = 4" (10 cm) in Stockinette st (St st)

Which Comes First: Purchased Sweater or Motif?

Inspiration for embellishment comes in all forms, and there's no right (or wrong) way for pairing a purchased item with a duplicate stitched motif. In the case of the Audrey Hepburn piece, designing the graph came first, but a pink boatneck sweater was an intuitive, perfect pairing for the motif.

If you're enraptured by a graphic motif but aren't quite sure where you'd like to place it, you may want to shop around for ideas. Know how many stitches and rows your purchased item needs to have in order to accommodate your graph. Also, have a sense for how varying gauges will affect the size of the finished motif. Carrying a tape measure and a calculator while shopping for a purchased item will allow you to check stitch counts, gauge, and placement before committing to it.

Embellishment
You do not need to knit a new garment or accessory from the ground up to take advantage of the graphs included in this book. Any graph can be incorporated into a purchased item, such as a sweater, tote bag, scarf, hat—truly, the sky is the limit.

Planning
The purchased item needs to be wide enough and tall (or long) enough to accommodate the graph you would like to apply. The Audrey Hepburn graph is 50 sts wide and 57 rows long; the sweater we purchased provides an ample canvas upon which to place this graph.

Determine the desired placement of your graph. This graphic portrait in particular lends itself to an off-center orientation, abutting the wide, ribbed hem of the sweater. For larger motifs, you may want to mark the intended "canvas" for your duplicate st, by basting a wide running st with a tapestry needle threaded with waste yarn, or by laying lengths of masking tape along the edge of your "canvas."

Duplicate Stitching

Following the technique instructions for duplicate stitching (page 143), begin applying the graphic motif to the purchased sweater. Work with manageable lengths of yarn, about 2' to 3' (0.6 to 0.9 m) long. Just as in graphic knitting, one square of the graph equals one V-shaped duplicate st. Monitor your tension as you build the motif: too tight, the surface may pucker; too loose and gaps between the embellishment yarn and the item will appear. Leave tails of embellishment yarn loose; weave in the ends to finish.

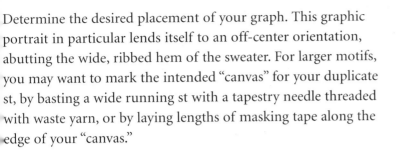

Mixology: Purchased Project with Embellishment

When applying duplicate stitch to a handknit project, as in the Moon Day Yoga Tank (page 120), you can easily select an embellishment yarn from the same line as your main yarn. However, when applying duplicate stitch to a purchased item, it is essential to match closely the gauge of the original piece to the new yarn. A yarn that is heftier will stretch and buckle the surface of the piece and appear warped, while a yarn that is lighter and thinner will lend a tweedy appearance.

Measure the gauge of the piece to be embellished the same as you would check a gauge swatch. Select an embellishment yarn that matches, or is a hair smaller, than the original piece. Instead of knitting a gauge swatch, embroider a short section to ensure you are achieving the desired tension and overall look. Keep color play, surface texture, stretch, and other elements in mind when planning your embellishment project.

Ditching yarn altogether and using embroidery floss will give you a smooth, satiny finish, and the palette available is almost endless.

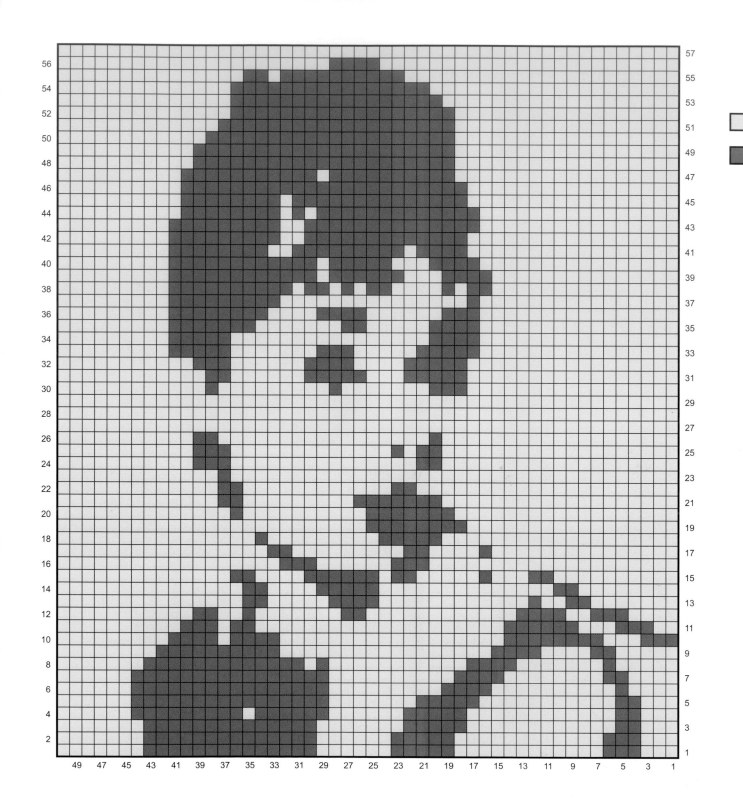

KEY

☐ MC

■ CC—
duplicate
stitch

appendix

Technique Library

The techniques illustrated here are used throughout the chapters of this book as the foundation elements of our featured colorwork.

Intarsia

Adding a second color of yarn in a row

1. Slide your right needle into the first stitch as if to knit (or purl, depending on where you are in your pattern). Lay the new color of yarn across the tip of the needle, leaving about a 6" (15 cm) tail hanging to the left, and the working yarn to the right.

2. Bring the working yarn around and underneath the old color, then wrap it around the needle to make a knit (or purl) stitch. Finish the stitch, dropping both the old loop and the tail of the new yarn over the newly formed stitch.

Changing colors in vertical stripes

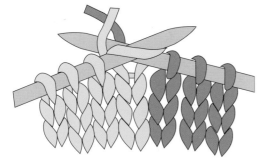

Step 1

1. On the knit side (WS), drop the old color.

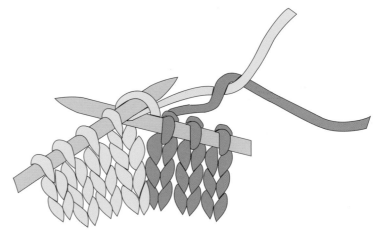

Step 2

2. Pick up the new color from under the old color and knit to the next color change

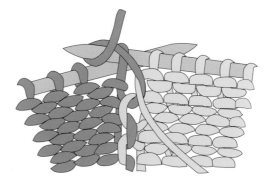

Step 3

3. On the purl side, drop the old color. Pick up the new color from under the old color and purl to the next color change. Repeat.

Fair Isle and Stranding

Stranding working yarn

Carried yarn should wrap the working yarn every two to three stitches in order to maintain a smooth fabric and prevent snags.

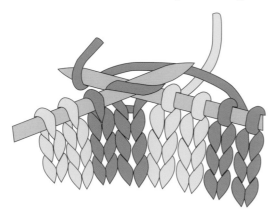

Step 1: Knit side

1. On the knit side, drop the working yarn. Bring the second color (now the working yarn) over the top of the dropped yarn and work to the next color change.

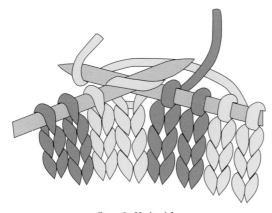

Step 2: Knit side

2. Drop the working yarn. Bring the second color under the dropped yarn and work to the next color change. Repeat for each color transition.

For stranding yarn on the purl side, simply change colors by bringing the second color yarn under the dropped yarn.

Twisting yarn

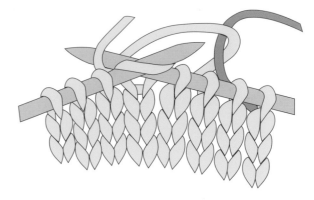

Knit side

On the knit side, twist the working yarn and the carried yarn around each other once. Continue knitting with the same color as before.

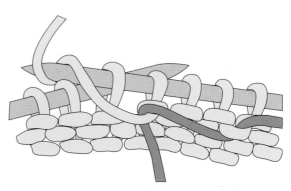

Purl side

On the purl side, twist the yarns around each other as shown, then continue purling with the same color as before.

Picking up stitches

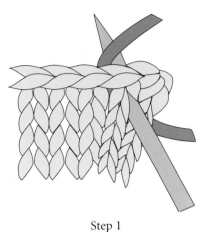

Step 1

1. With the front of the knitted piece facing you, insert a knitting needle through the center of a stitch at the far right edge of the desired design line, or where the new knit component should start. Wrap the yarn around the needle.

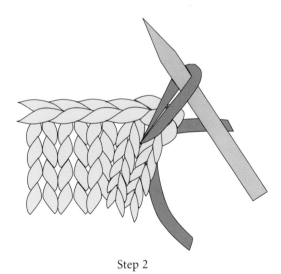

Step 2

2. Draw the new loop through the stitch to the front. Keep the loop on the needle and repeat these steps, working the needle into the next stitch to the left, one at a time, until the desired number of stitches have been picked up.

Embellishment Library

Unless otherwise indicated, you should use a yarn tapestry needle for all embroidery stitches. For best results and an even texture, choose embellishment yarns with a smooth surface and weave.

We've provided instructions for basic embroidery stitches here to get you started. There are innumerable sources of additional tips, techniques, and style inspiration for embroidery, including books, magazines, and websites.

Stem Stitch

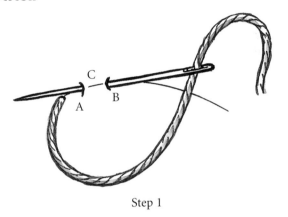

Step 1

1. Bring the thread to the front of the fabric on the left end of the design line (A). Hold down the thread with your left thumb, and insert the needle into the fabric slightly to the right on the design line (B). Bring the tip of the needle out midway between points A and B (C). Continue holding down the thread with your thumb as you pull the thread through to set the first stitch.

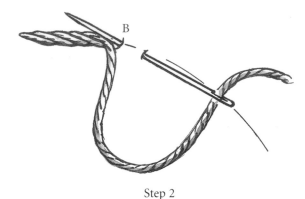

Step 2

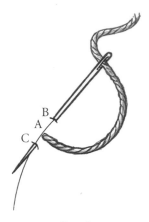

Step 2

2. Insert the needle into the fabric on the design line slightly to the right of point B. Bring the needles to the front again at B (in exactly the same hole). Hold the thread down with your left thumb and pull the thread through to set the second stitch. Continue working the embroidery in this way, trying to make all the stitches about the same length. To tie off, take the needle to the back at the end of the design line. Anchor the thread with three or four small loop knots.

2. Insert the needle into the fabric at the right end of the design line (B). Bring the tip of the needle out to the left of A (C) on the design line. Pull the thread through to set the first stitch.

Back Stitch

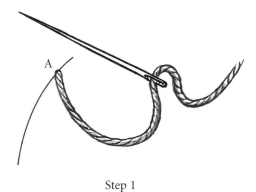

Step 1

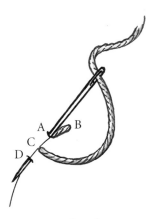

Step 3

1. Bring the thread to the front of the fabric a short distance from the right end of the design line (A).

3. Reinsert the needle into the fabric at A (in exactly the same hole). Bring the tip of the needle out to the left of C (D) on the design line. Pull the thread through to set the second stitch. Continue working the embroidery in this way, trying to make all the stitches about the same length.

Interlaced Backstitch

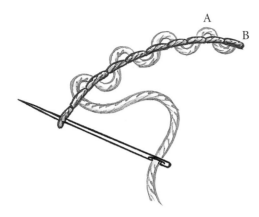

1. Work the backstitch along the design line and tie off.

2. Thread a tapestry needle with the same or contrasting yarn or thread. Bring the needle to the front of the fabric under the first stitch at the right of the backstitched design line (between A and B). Weave the needle in and out, alternately, under the backstitches. Take care not to pierce either the fabric or the backstitch threads.

Straight Stitch

Bring the needle to the front of the fabric (A). Insert the needle back into the fabric (B) for the desired stitch length, and then bring it out at the beginning of the next stitch (C). Straight stitches can be worked uniformly or irregularly, depending on the effect you wish to achieve. To tie off, take the needle to the back on the last stitch. Anchor the thread with three or four small loop knots.

Padded Satin Stitch/Satin Stitch

Follow all four steps for a padded satin stitch. For small shapes that don't require padding, omit step 2. For a plain satin stitch, omit steps 1 and 2 and simply embroider from edge to edge to fill the designated area.

Step 1

1. Backstitch around the outline of the shape.

Step 2

2. Fill the shape with tiny straight stitches that run perpendicular to the direction in which the satin stitch will be worked. (This type of filling is called "seeding.")

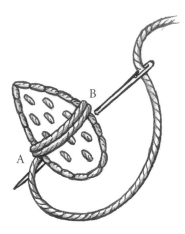

Step 3

3. Begin at the widest part of the shape. Bring the needle to the front just outside the backstitched outline (A). Pull the needle through, and take it to the back on the opposite side (B), angling the needle under the outline. Continue working satin stitches close together until half the shape is covered.

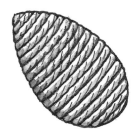

Step 4

4. Begin at the widest part again to work satin stitches over the remainder of the shape. The padded satin stitch is now complete
To tie off, take the needle to the back and carefully weave the tail through the threads on the underside of the satin-stitched shape.

Lazy Daisy Stitch

Step 1   Step 2

1. Bring the needle to the front of the fabric at A. Reinsert the needle into the fabric at A (in exactly the same hole), and then bring the needle back up at B.

2. Loop the thread counterclockwise so it passes under the needle. Push the needle through the fabric. Hold the thread loop lightly with your left thumb, and pull the needle gently away from you. Release the thread from your left thumb as the loop decreases in size.

Step 3   Step 4

3. Continue pulling the thread away from you until the loop lies flat against the surface of the fabric.

4. To anchor the stitch, take the needle to the back of the fabric just over the looped thread.

Chain Stitch

Chain stitch is actually a continuous row of lazy daisy stitches. Begin by working steps 1 through 3 for the lazy daisy (but don't anchor the stitch as instructed in step 4).

Step 5

5. Reinsert the needle into the fabric at B (in exactly the same hole). Bring the needle back out at point C to finish the first stitch and start the second stitch.

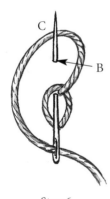

Step 6

6. Continue working the embroidery in this way, trying to make each stitch equal in length.

To tie off, insert the needle into the fabric just over the looped thread and take it to the back (lazy daisy stitch, step 4). Anchor the thread with three or four small loop knots.

Blanket Stitch

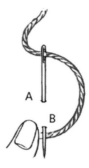

Step 1

1. Bring the needle to the front of the knitted fabric. Holding the yarn down with your left thumb, insert the needle into the fabric at A and come back out at B. Continue holding the yarn down as you pull the needle through the fabric and over the working yarn.

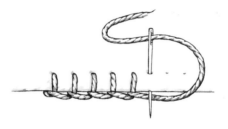

Step 2

2. Repeat the step 1 motion, leaving the desired amount of space between stitches. To tie off, take the needle to the back on the last stitch at the end of the design line. Anchor the yarn and weave in the end.

French Knot

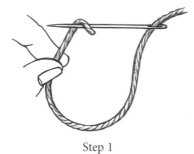

Step 1

1. Bring the needle to the front of the fabric at the place where the knot is to be positioned. Hold the thread taut between your left thumb and index finger, approximately 1" (2.5 cm) from the surface of the fabric.

Step 2

2. Using your left hand, wrap the thread once around the needle.

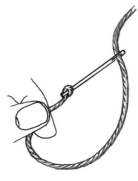

Step 3

3. Hold the thread taut again, and insert the point of the needle into the fabric one or two threads away from the starting point. Push the needle to the back of the fabric, all the while holding the thread down with your left thumb. Release your thumb as you pull the thread to the back to set the French knot.

Step 4

4. A completed French knot. For a more prominent knot, wrap the yarn twice or even three times in step 2.

Duplicate Stitch

Duplicate stitch is only worked on stockinette fabric, and is best applied with a yarn whose gauge matches that of the finished fabric. Using a tapestry needle threaded with yarn, secure the end of the yarn to the back of the knitted fabric near a convenient starting point in your planned design.

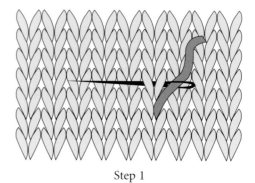

Step 1

1. Bring the needle up through the point of the first stitch to be worked and insert it behind the point of the stitch above it.

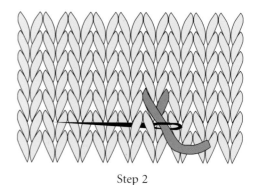

Step 2

2. Pull the needle down through the first point and bring it up through the point of the next stitch.

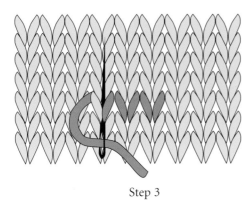

Step 3

3. To begin the next row, insert the needle into the base of the stitch directly above the last stitch made.

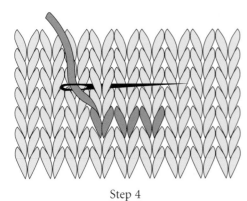

Step 4

4. Repeat this stitch as you did on the previous row.

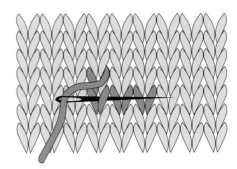

Step 5

5. To complete the first stitch on this row, insert your needle behind threads that have already been stitched.

When working with duplicate stitch, it is easier and much neater to work the stitches that are either side-by-side or directly above or below. There should not be any stranded or crisscrossing lines in the back of the work unless it is absolutely necessary. Not only does this keep your work neat, it prevents the color from showing through from the back. It also prevents potential snagging later on.

Single Crochet along the Edge

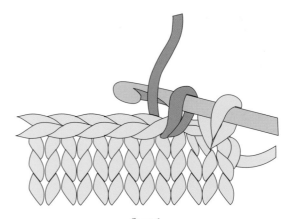

Step 1

1. Draw through a loop as for a slip stitch, then bring the yarn over the hook and pull it through the first loop. Insert the hook into the next stitch and draw through a second loop.

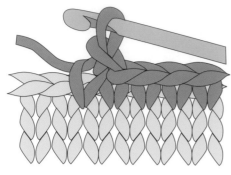

Step 2

2. Yarn over and pull through both loops on the hook. Reinsert the hook into the next stitch, draw through a second loop, and repeat steps along the desired design line.

I-Cord

With double-pointed needles and specified yarn, CO the desired number of stitches. Knit 1 row. *Do not turn.* Slide the stitches to the right end of the needle, pull the yarn taut around the back, and knit the stitches, cinching the working yarn to close the cord. Repeat process for the desired length of the I-cord. BO all sts.

Attached I-Cord

With double-pointed needles and specified yarn, CO the desired number of stitches. Knit 1 row. *Do not turn.* ✳ Slide the sts to the right end of the needle and knit the sts again, then pick up a st from the edge to which you want to attach your I-Cord. Slide the sts to the right end of the needle. Knit 2 sts, k2tog, then knit to end. Slide the sts to the right end of the needle. Knit the sts again. Repeat from ✳ until you have worked the required length of I-Cord.

Twisted Cord

Step 1   Step 2

1. Cut several lengths of yarn that measure about five times the desired finished cord length. Fold the strands in half to form two equal sections. Anchor the strands at the fold by looping them over a doorknob. Holding one section in each hand, twist each section tightly in one direction until they begin to kink.

2. Put both sections in one hand, then release them, allowing them to twist around and embrace each other. Smooth out the twists so they are uniform; knot the ends to secure.

gallery of graphs

In order to fit as many graphs as possible, some run smaller than others. We suggest photocopying and enlarging any of these graphs as needed.

Fleur-de-lis

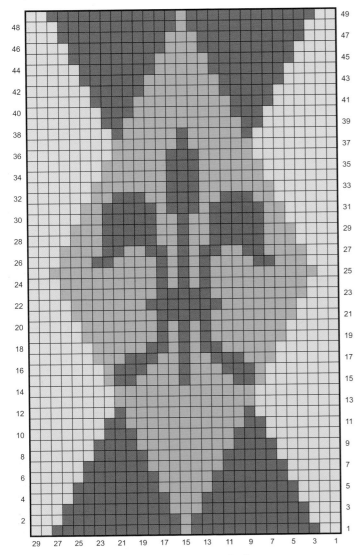

Repeat vertically or horizontally for pattern

Zigzag / Herringbone

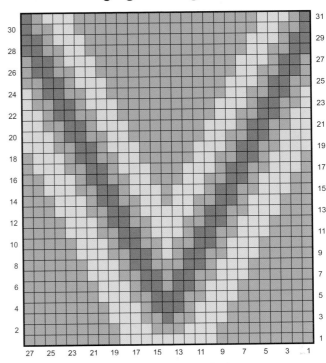

Repeat vertically or horizontally for pattern

Zodiac Symbols
Alternate graphs; Baby, What's Your Sign?
Zodiac Socks, page 114

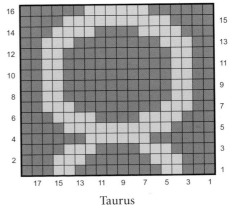

Taurus

Zodiac Symbols, continued

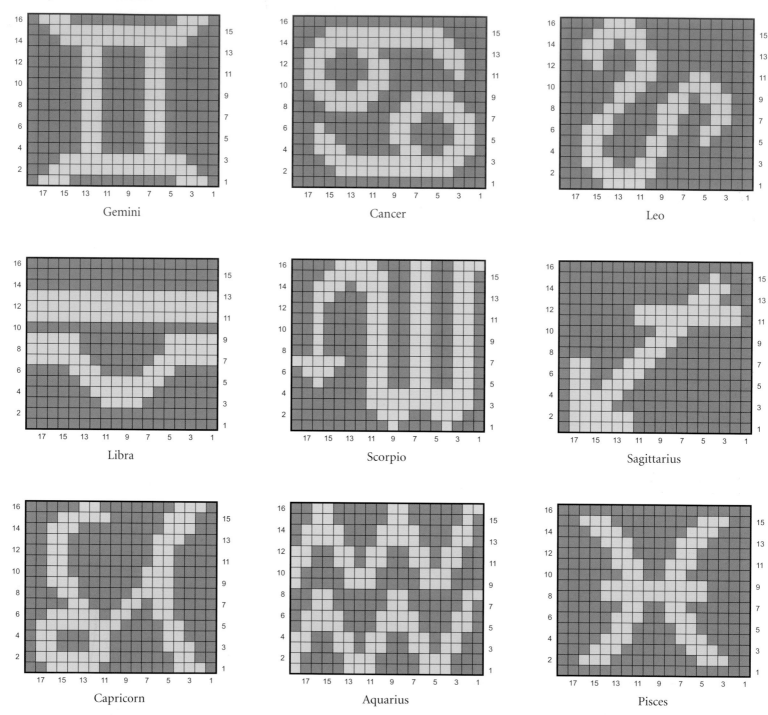

Gemini

Cancer

Leo

Libra

Scorpio

Sagittarius

Capricorn

Aquarius

Pisces

Celtic Knot

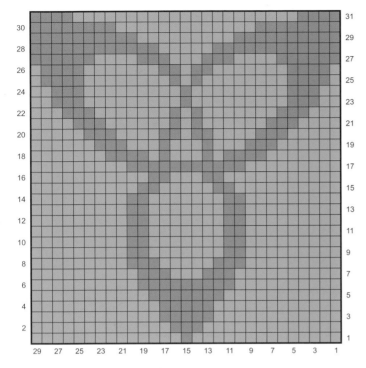

Eight Ball

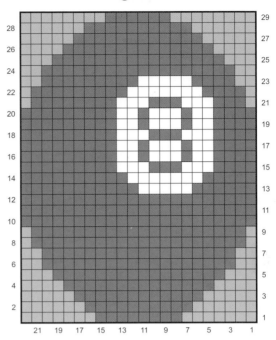

Abstract Matrix

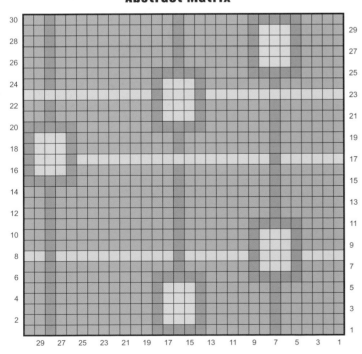

Diamond

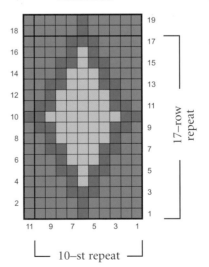

17–row repeat

10–st repeat

Repeat vertically or horizontally for pattern

Peacock

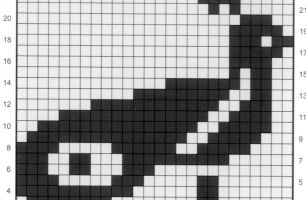

Dragonfly

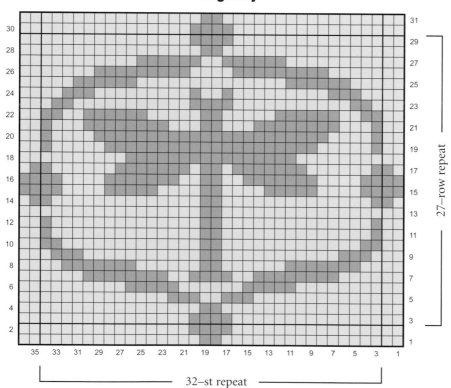

32–st repeat

27–row repeat

Eiffel Tower

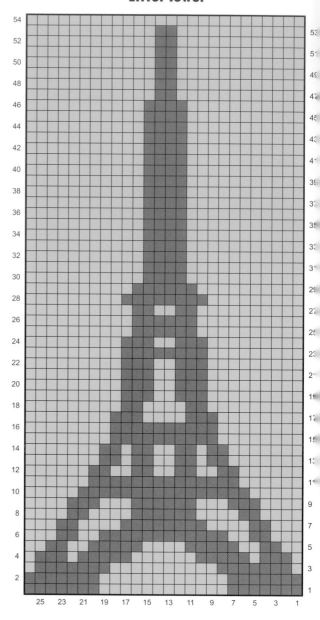

Fair Isle Greek Key

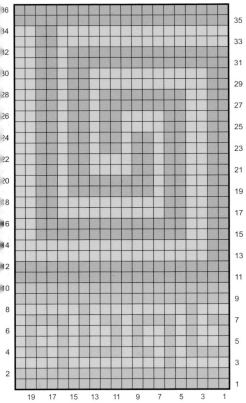

Henna Motif 1

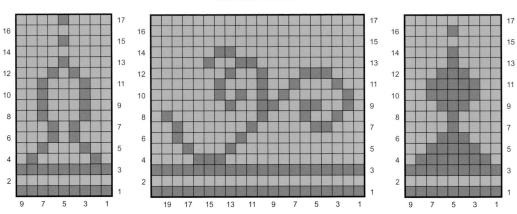

Lotus 1

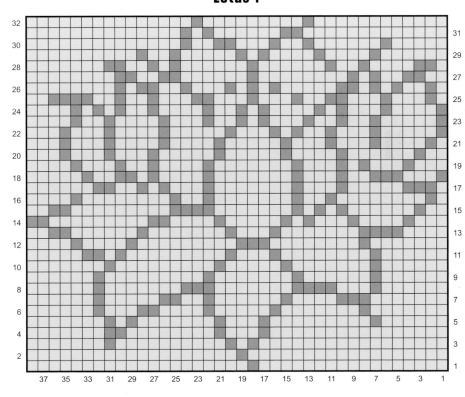

Poodle

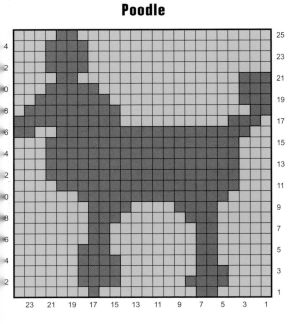

Fair Isle Spirals

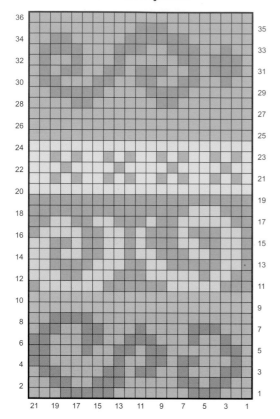

Henna Motif 2

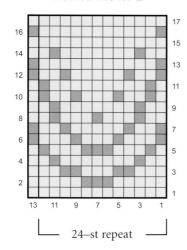

24–st repeat

Lotus 2

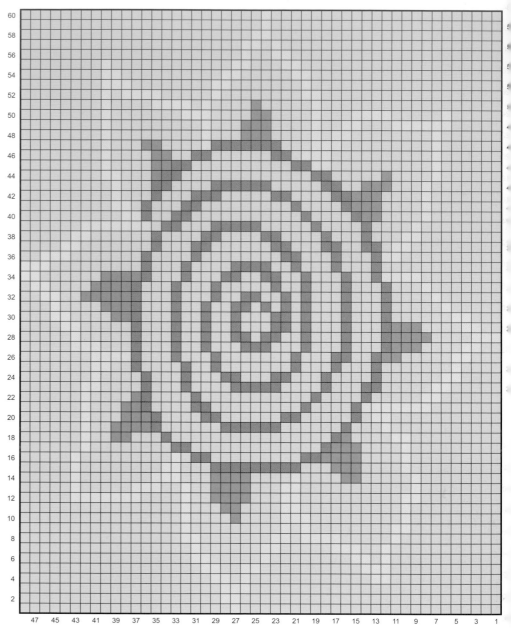

Star

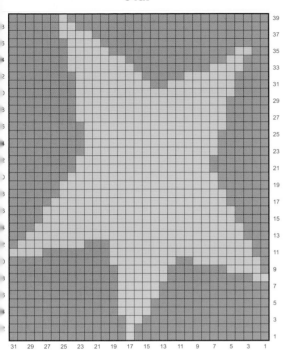

Spiral

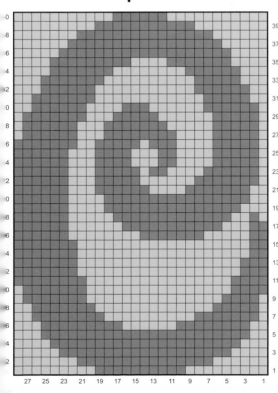

Script Alphabet

Aa Bb Cc Dd
Ee Ff Gg Hh
Ii Jj Kk Ll
Mm Nn Oo Pp
Qq Rr Ss Tt
Uu Vv Ww
Xx Yy Zz

Alphabet

**Alternate graphs;
Monogrammed Handbag,
page 44**

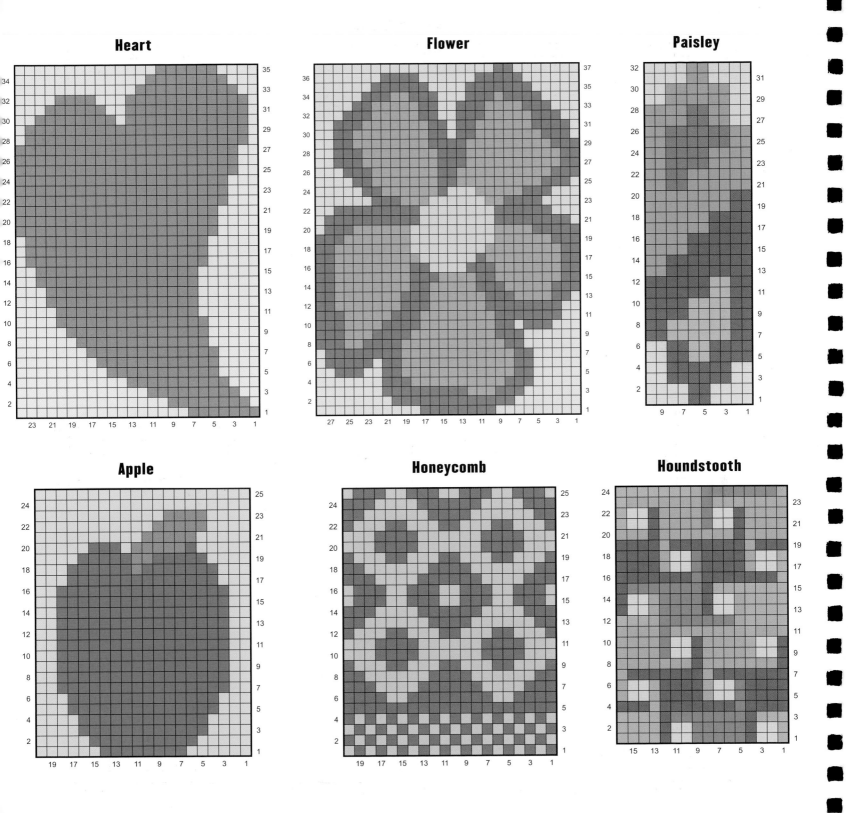

Birth of Venus

Cherries
Alternate Graph, Pear Amour Leg Warmers, page 90

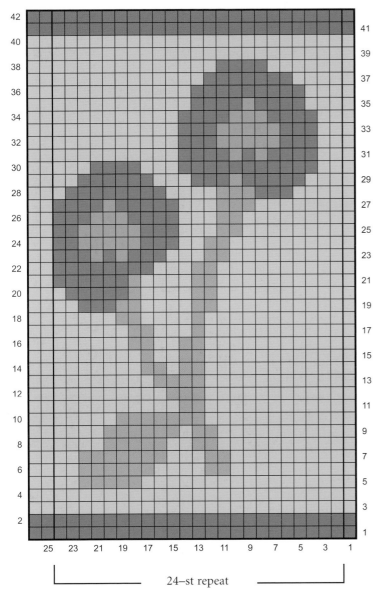

24–st repeat

Repeat motif three times for pattern.

Flames

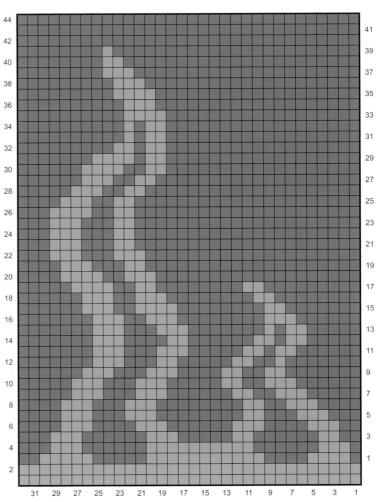

resources

Halcyon Yarn
12 School Street
Bath, ME 04530 USA
800.341.0282
Service@halcyonyarn.com
www.halcyonyarn.com
Supplier of Casco Bay Worsted cotton

Himilaya Yarn Company
129 Mallard Drive
Colchester, VT 05446 USA
802.862.6985
www.himalayayarn.com
Supplier of Himalaya Wool/Silk, Rayon, and Recycled Silk

JoAnn Fabrics
www.joann.com
Fabrics, pillow forms, buttons

Knit One, Crochet Too, Inc.
91 Tandberg Trail, Unit 6
Windham, ME 04062 USA
207.892.9903
www.knitonecrochettoo.com
Supplier of Wick, Paint Box, and Parfait yarns

Knitting Fever
P.O. Box 336
315 Bayview Avenue
Amityville, NY 11701 USA
516.546.3600
www.knittingfever.com
Distributor of Araucania Nature Wool Worsted

Patons
320 Livingstone Avenue South
Listowel, ON N4W 3H3
Canada
888.368.8401
www.patonsyarns.com
Classic merino wool

Portland Fiber Gallery
229 Congress Street
Portland, ME 04101 USA
207.780.1345
Glass buttons by artist Gordy Thomas

Twisted Sisters Knitting
740 Metcalf Street
Escondido, CA 92025 USA
760.489.8846
Hand-dyed and hand-painted yarns

Westminster Fibers, Inc.
4 Townsend West, Suite 8
Nashua, NH 03063 USA
603.886.5041
info@westminsterfibers.com
or www.knitrowan.com
Supplier of Rowan, Nashua, Jaeger, and Gedifra yarns

contributors

Nicky Epstein

Nicky Epstein is a prolific and versatile knitwear designer, author, and teacher, and her designs are

page 68

featured in knitting magazines and publications, on television, and in museums. She is the author of *Knitting On the Edge, Knitting Over the Edge, Nicky Epstein's Knitted Flowers, Knitting Beyond the Edge,* and *Nicky Epstein's Fabulous Felted Bags.*

Mercedes Tarasovich-Clark

Knit Nouveau, Inc.
4094 Helena Road
Helena, AL 35080
USA
205.664.5858
mercedes@knitnouveau.com
www.knitnouveau.com

page 78

Mercedes Tarasovich-Clark runs Knit Nouveau, a yarn shop outside of Birmingham, Alabama. She enjoys using her colorwork background in textile arts to create fresh color combinations for herself and her customers.

Natalie Wilson

iKnitiative, LLC
12948 Victoria Avenue
Huntington Woods,
 MI 48070 USA
248.586.0350
natalie@iknitiative.com
www.iknitiative.com

page 48

Natalie Wilson is a knitwear designer and knitting teacher working out of the Detroit area. Her designs have appeared in many publications including *Interweave Knits* and *Knitter's Magazine.* Her iKnitiative line of patterns is sold at fine yarn shops throughout North America.

Anni Kristensen

Himalaya Yarns
anni@himalayayarn.com

Anni was born and raised in a small Danish village with two passions in life—to knit and to travel the world. In late 1996, her two passions merged into Himalaya Yarn, a company that provides hand-knitting yarns for the North American market using the technology available in Nepal.

page 26

Stewart Watkins

The Yarn Lounge
3003 West Cary Street
Richmond, VA 23221
USA
804.340.2880
stewart@theyarnlounge.com
www.theyarnlounge.com

page 124

Stewart Watkins opened the Yarn Lounge in Richmond, Virginia, in March 2005. He holds a master of fine art degree in photography.

Cecelia Wu

wucecelia@yahoo.com

Cecelia loves to knit and, more important to design, because of her inability to follow instructions. She works in health care policy and spends much of her free time, and some of her work time, knitting or thinking about knitting.

page 82

acknowledgments

Special thanks to Kelly Speakman of Somerville, Massachusetts, who knit the body of the Monogrammed Clutch (and who, thus, got to have her initial immortalized); to Becky Zimmerman of Salem, Massachusetts, who contributed her exquisite knitting skills, patience, and eye for detail to Ella's Mom's Argyle Mittens; to Margarita Mejia of Forest Hills, New York, who whipped up our Jon Stewart portrait in a cinch; and to Cecelia Wu (Ella's "mom" herself), who not only knit the Tribal Sun Messenger Bag, but who served as test audience, design consultant, constructive critic, and overall partner in crime, throughout the creation of this book.

Thank you to Mary Ann Hall and Winnie Prentiss, two of Rockport's chicks with sticks (and hooks), who saw the promise for this project and paved the way for its development; and to Lisa Evans, whose studio is the proverbial candy store, and whose design savvy actualized this project. —R.B.

Special thanks to Greta Roderick, my dear friend who knows how to calculate pi in her head and always makes me laugh. Thank you for being so willing and able to help me bring my ideas to reality (and for knitting so fast); also to Ken Bridgewater of Westminster Fibers for his support in so many ways, not the least of which is his generous contribution of the Nashua, Rowan, and Jaeger yarns for this book.

Thank you to Hélène Rush of Knit One, Crochet Too for her contribution of the really cool yarn, Wick, and the beautiful Paint Box and Parfait yarns; to Anni Kristensen of Himalaya Yarn Company for her contribution of the lovely handspun wool, silk, and rayon yarns which are a delight to work with; to Catherine Shumadine, a truly modern knitter who patiently knitted the Fire and Ice Men's Pullover, via email installments of the pattern; and to my lovely sister-in-law, Mika Christian Bailey, thank you for indulging me and allowing me to rummage through your amazing stash of fabric.

Thank you to Mary Ann Hall for inviting me to participate in the creation of this book and to Rochelle Bourgault for being such a fun and hip coauthor. —L.B.E.

about the authors

Rochelle Bourgault is a project manager at Rockport Publishers and Quarry Books, a freelance writer, and an all-around crafty gal. A graduate of Dartmouth College with a degree in English literature and creative writing, she attempted her first knitting project at the age of eight, and has come a long way from that ill-fated slipper. She lives in Cambridge, Massachusetts.

Lisa B. Evans is a landscape architect, devoted knitter, and mother of three. She has designed for the needlecraft industry for more than 15 years, and started her own business, LB Evans Handknits, in 2001 with an innovative line of knitted handbags, backpacks, and totes. She currently is a design consultant to Westminster Fibers, Inc. She leads knitting workshops and retreats, and assists the handwork instructors at her children's school, the Merriconeag Waldorf School in Freeport, Maine.

You may not be able to judge a book by its cover, but you can gauge a knitter's style savvy by her needle case. This felted case begins as a rectangle, and can be sewn into any number of configurations depending on what you need to stow away, whether it be knitting needles or an MP3 player. The ribbon ties can easily be modified, and any length of fabric or fiber, including a complementary felted I-cord, can be substituted for the ribbon.

Designer: Rochelle Bourgault

Finished Size

Before felting: $23^{1}/_{2}$" × $22^{3}/_{4}$" (59.7 × 57.8 cm)
After felting: $18^{1}/_{2}$" × 17" (47 × 43.2 cm)

Materials

Yarn

Medium, worsted-weight wool/alpaca blend

Shown: Nashua Creative Focus Worsted (75% wool / 25% alpaca, 220 yds (200 m) / (100 g), #2025 Syrah (MC), #2095 Cayenne (CC).

Needles

One size 7 (4.5 mm) straight needles, one pair, 14" (34.4 cm) long

Notions

Matching sewing thread and sewing machine or needle; 2 yards (1.8 m) 1" (2.5 cm) -wide contrasting satin ribbon

Gauge

Gauge 20 sts and 28 rows = 4" (10 cm) in Stockinette st (St st) before felting

Always check your gauge! Adjust needle size to obtain correct gauge if necessary.

Needle Case

With MC, CO 118 sts. Begin St st. Work even for 36 rows, ending on WS row. ✱ Next Row (RS): Establish pattern: K5, work graphic motif from chart across center 110 sts, using the intarsia method when switching colors (see page 136), k3. Work 34 rows of chart. ✱ With MC, work in St st for 4 rows. Next Row (RS): Repeat between ✱ once. With MC, work in St st for 10 rows. Next Row (RS): With MC, k5, change to CC and k98, change to MC and k5. Continuing in St st and color pattern as established, work even until piece measures 21³/₄"

KEY

☐ St st—knit on RS, purl on WS

▪ MC

▪ CC

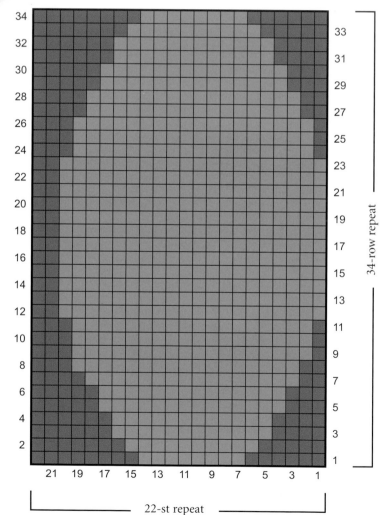

(55.2 cm), ending on WS row. Next Row (RS): With MC, work in St st for 7 rows. BO all sts knitwise.

Follow instructions for felting (right). Block project to desired measurements and let air dry.

Finishing

With WS of felted fabric facing up, and rows of circles at the top, fold up a 7$\frac{1}{2}$" (19.1 cm) flap, creating inside pocket. With sewing machine or needle and sewing thread, sew edges of case together. Determine desired width of pockets (1" [2.5 cm] wide for smaller size needles, up to 3" [7.6 cm] wide for larger size needles), and stitch parallel seams for pockets. Begin each seam about $\frac{1}{2}$" (1.3 cm) up from bottom edge of fold and end each seam just before the BO edge.

Attaching the Ribbon Ties: Fold ribbon in half and sew in place halfway between top and bottom edges of case, about 6" (15.2 cm) in from one edge or along one of the needle pocket seams.

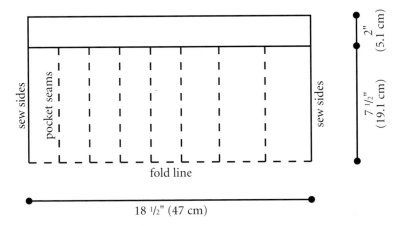

Note: Measurements given are after felting.

Felting Instructions

Thread a tapestry needle and weave in all loose yarn tails to the wrong side of the work. Partially fill a washing machine with hot water. Add a small amount of mild detergent or dishwashing liquid (too many suds will hamper the felting process). Place the item to be felted in an enclosed pillowcase. Use a separate pillowcase for smaller pieces, such as straps, pockets, and so on, to avoid tangles. Place the pillowcase(s) in the washer. (You may add a heavy pair of jeans or sneakers to increase agitation and aid in the felting process. Note: If your yarn is not colorfast, other items may be discolored in the process.) Set the washing machine at its longest and hottest wash cycle.

Check the felting process frequently (every five minutes). Monitoring the project is crucial, as it is difficult to stretch and reshape a project that has shrunken too small. Reset the wash cycle as needed until all items are felted satisfactorily. Felting usually takes several repetitions; the process is complete when the stitches are obscured and the fabric is firm. Turn the washer to the spin cycle to remove excess water. Stretch bags and hats over suitable forms. Felted items should fit their forms snugly. Mold, pull, and poke the fabric until the desired shape or size is obtained. Hang straps and smaller pieces to dry. Allow your felted piece to completely air dry. (Note: Superwash wools and synthetic yarns will not felt.)

Hand Felting Variation
To felt small items by hand, fill a dishpan or sink with hot, almost boiling water, add a little liquid dishwashing soap, and vigorously rub all parts of the item until the fabric becomes dense and it is difficult or impossible to see individual stitches. Rinse well several times to remove any soapy residue. Shape the item and allow it to air dry.

It *Is* Easy Being Green Monogrammed Handbag

In the beginning, there was a rectangle. Shortly thereafter, there were multitudes of simple knit accessories whipped up from these rectangles. An intarsia monogram anchors the front panel of this piece, while a chunky I-cord and leaf cluster transform it into a functional, personalized, and peerless handbag.

Designer: Rochelle Bourgault

Finished Dimensions
Clutch (before assembly)
Before Felting: 10" × 15³/₄" (25.4 × 40 cm)
After Felting: approximately 9" × 13" (22.9 × 32.5 cm)

I-Cord Straps
Before Felting: 40" (101.6 cm)
After Felting: approximately 33" (83.8 cm)

Materials
Yarn
Medium, worsted-weight wool/alpaca blend

Shown: Nashua Handknits Creative Focus Worsted (75% wool / 25% alpaca; 220 yards [201.2 m] / 100 g): #3864 Bud Green, 2 balls (MC); #0410 Espresso, 1 ball (CC)

Needles
One pair size 10¹/₂ (6.5 mm) straight needles, 14" (34.4 cm) long; one pair size 10¹/₂ double-pointed needles (dpn)

Notions
I/9 (5.5 mm) crochet hook; stitch markers; tapestry needle; sewing needle; matching embroidery thread

Gauge

16 sts and 20 rows = 4" (10 cm) in Stockinette st (St st) with two strands of yarn held together

Always check your gauge! Adjust needle size to obtain correct gauge if necessary.

Clutch

With straight needles and two strands of MC held together, CO 40 stitches. Beg St st. Work even for 50 rows (piece should measure approximately 10" [25.4 cm] from CO edge).

Beg monogram from chart as follows: Work 5 sts, place marker (pm), work across row 1 from chart, pm, work to end. Work all 23 rows of chart. (Note: You may adjust placement of your monogram by working more or fewer sts before beginning chart.)

(WS) Continuing with MC and St st (beg with a purl row), work even for 6 rows. BO all sts.

Strap

With dpn and two strands of MC held together, CO 8 sts. Work I-cord (see page 145) for 40" (101.6 cm). BO all sts.

Felted Three-Leaf Closure
Leaf (make three)

Leaf pattern adapted from Nicky Epstein's Knitting Over the Edge *(Sixth & Spring Books, 2005)*

With dpn and two strands of MC held together, CO 5 sts.
Row 1 (RS): K2, yo, k1, yo, k2—7 sts.
Row 2 and all WS rows: purl.
Row 3 K3, yo, k1, yo, k3—9 sts.
Row 5 K4, yo, k1, yo, k4—11 sts.
Row 7 Ssk, k7, k2tog—9 sts rem.
Row 9 Ssk, k5, k2tog—7 sts rem.
Row 11 Ssk, k3, k2tog—5 sts rem.
Row 13 Ssk, k1, k2tog—3 sts rem.
Row 15 Sl 1, k2tog, psso—1 st rem.
Fasten off.

Loop Closure

With crochet hook and single strand of MC, work 8" (20.3 cm) crochet chain. Fasten off.

Notes To personalize your clutch, see page 152–153 for charts graphing every *other* letter of the alphabet.

Finishing

Weave in loose ends to WS and secure.

Felting: Felt all pieces using your desired method (see page 43), until all components are of desired dimensions. Body of clutch should measure approximately 13" × 9" (33 × 22.9 cm) and strap should be approximately 33" (83.8 cm) after felting. The specific dimensions of felted leaves are less essential; the ones shown are approximately 2" × 2½" (5.1 × 6.4 cm). The loop should be just long enough to keep clutch closed, approximately 6" (15.2 cm).

Embroidered Detail (optional): With tapestry needle and 24" (61 cm) of CC, work slightly curving backstitch (see page 140) up center of each leaf to add contrasting detail.

With tapestry needle and 12" (30.5 cm) of matching embroidery thread, stack leaves in desired arrangement and tack them together at their base. Center leaf arrangement along top edge of front of clutch, and tack it down with embroidery thread.

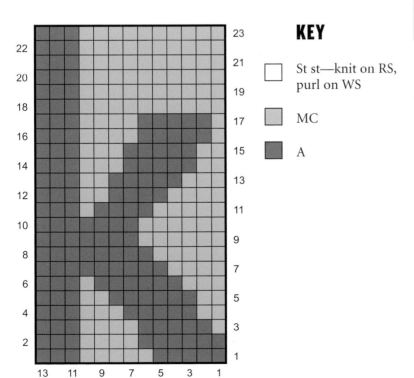

KEY

☐	St st—knit on RS, purl on WS
☐	MC
☐	A

Design Variations

✳ Change the dimensions of the rectangle, or alter the fold and assembly lines. Create a wide clutch with a flap, a wallet-sized pouch, or even a cell-phone cozy, simply by adjusting the rectangle's measurements, and the scale and orientation of the I-cord and closures.

✳ Expand the monogram. Use letters from the alphabets included (in the Gallery of Graphs, page 146), or modify your own, to create a two- or three-letter monogram.

✳ Embroider additional details, in any number of colors of scrap yarn, throughout the finished project. (Hint: Felted fabric makes an excellent canvas, and unfelted embroidered details retain their crispness better than felted.)

✳ Drop the leaves in favor of a knit flower, purchased button, or any closure your heart—or style—desires.

Center felted loop on inside top edge on back of clutch, and tack it down with yarn threaded on a tapestry needle. The loop must fit easily around leaf cluster in order to work properly as a closure.

The strap forms sides of clutch. Fold clutch in half; center one end of strap over fold line at one edge and pin it in place. Pin front and back of clutch to sides of strap. With tapestry needle and approximately 36" (91.4 cm) of CC, use blanket St (see page 143) to sew strap to clutch. Twist strap five to seven times. Repeat for opposite side.

The Butterfly Effect Cardigan

When this cleverly designed cardigan flutters its wings, a knitter scores a fresh interpretation of intarsia work. This pattern offers two distinct styles: the two symmetrical butterfly halves can meet in a subtle hook-and-eye closure, as shown, or they can just as easily be stitched together. Both options retain the cutaway bottom detail, while the latter turns the cardigan into a pullover.

Designer: Natalie Wilson

Sizes
Small (Medium, Large)
Model shown in size Small.

Finished Dimensions
Chest: 36 (40½, 44)" (91.4 [102.9, 111.8] cm)

Materials
Yarn
Light-weight wool blend

Shown: Rowan Felted Tweed (50% merino wool / 25% alpaca / 25% viscose/rayon, 191 yards [174.7 m]/ 50 g): #151 Bilberry (MC), 6 (6, 7) balls; #152 Watery (A), #146 Herb (B), and #150 Rage (C), 1 ball each

Needles
One pair size 6 (4 mm) straight needles, or one size 6 circular needle, 24" (61 cm) long

Notions
E/4 (3.5 mm) crochet hook, row counter, tapestry needle, hook and eye closure

Gauge
23 sts and 32 rows = 4" (10 cm) in Stockinette Stitch (St st)

Always check your gauge! Adjust needle size to obtain correct gauge if necessary.

Back
With MC and provisional CO method, CO 104 (116, 126) sts. Work in St st, beg with a purl row, for 19 rows.

Body Shaping
Decrease 1 st each edge this row, then every 6 rows 5 times—92 (104, 114) sts. Work even for 15 rows. Increase 1 st each edge this row, then every 6 rows 5 times—104 (116, 126) sts. Work even until piece measures 13" (32.5 cm) or desired length to under-arm, ending with a WS row.

Armhole Shaping
BO 5 (6, 7) sts at beg of next 2 rows, then decrease 1 st each edge every 5 rows 4 times—84 (94, 102) sts. Work even until armhole measures 8 (8½, 9)" (20.3 [21.6, 22.9] cm) or the desired arm-hole length, ending with a WS row.

Shoulder and Neck Shaping
BO 4 (5, 6) sts, k25 (29, 32), attach second ball, BO off center 26 sts, knit to end. BO 4 (5, 6) sts at beg of next 9 (7, 7) rows, then 3 (4, 4) sts at beg of next 2 (4, 4) rows, and at the same time, dec 1 st at each neck edge every row 6 times.

Right Front

With MC and provisional CO method (see page 39), CO 38 (42, 46) sts. Work in St st, beg with a purl row, for 2 rows.

Body Shaping

Increase 1 st at beg of row every other row 16 times and, AT THE SAME TIME, decrease 1 st at the end of row 20, then every 6 rows 5 times—48 (52, 56) sts. Work even for 15 rows.

Begin Chart

Work row 1 of chart A over 28 sts using intarsia method. Place marker (pm), work to end, increase 1 st at end of row—49 (53, 57) sts. Continue as est, placing markers for butterfly body as indicated in chart. Increase 1 st at end of row every 6 rows 5 times—54 (58, 62) sts. Work even until row 47 of chart is complete.

Armhole Shaping

BO 5 (6, 7) sts at beg of armhole edge. Decrease 1 st at beg of armhole edge every 4 rows 5 times—44 (47, 50) sts rem. The chart should now be complete. Remove chart marker.

Neck Shaping

Decrease 1 st at neck edge this row, every other row 20 (15, 12) times, then every 4 rows 0 (3, 5) times—23 (28, 32) sts rem. Work even until piece measures same as back to shoulder shaping, ending with a RS row.

Shoulder

BO 4 (5, 6) sts at armhole edge 5 (4, 4) times, then 3 (4, 4) sts 1 (2, 2) times.

Left Front

With MC, CO 38 (42, 46) sts. Work in St st, beg with a purl row, for 2 rows.

Body Shaping

Increase 1 st at end of row every other row 16 times and, at the same time, decrease 1 st at beg of row 20, then every 6 rows 5 times—48 (52, 56) sts. Work even for 15 rows.

Begin Chart

Increase 1 st at beg of row, work 20 (24, 28) sts, pm, work row 1 of chart B to end—49 (53, 57) sts. Continue as est, placing markers for butterfly body as indicated in chart. Increase 1 st at beg of row every 6 rows 5 times—54 (58, 62) sts. Work even until row 46 of chart is complete.

Armhole Shaping

BO 5 (6, 7) sts at beg of armhole edge. Decrease 1 st at beg of armhole edge every 4 rows 5 times—44 (47, 50) sts rem. Work even for 1 row. Chart should now be complete. Remove chart marker.

Neck Shaping

Decrease 1 st at neck edge this row, every other row 20 (15, 12) times, then every 4 rows 0 (3, 5) times—23 (28, 32) sts remain. Work even until piece measures same as back to shoulder shaping, ending with a WS row.

Shoulder Shaping

BO 4 (5, 6) sts at armhole edge 5 (4, 4) times, then 3 (4, 4) sts 1 (2, 2) times.

Sleeves (make two)

With MC and provisional CO method, CO 60 (62, 64) sts. Work in St st, beg with a purl row, for 9 rows.

Design Variation

* Know a lepidopterist who'll demand species-specific precision in her choices of butterflies? Modify the wing yarns and colors to attain zoological accuracy. (Add a dose of sauciness by embroidering the Latin nomenclature along the hem.)

Sleeve Shaping

Decrease 1 st each edge this row, then every 8 rows twice—54 (56, 58) sts remain. Work even for 7 rows. Increase 1 st each edge this row, every 8 rows 4 (9, 12) times, then every 10 rows 6 (2, 0) times—76 (80, 84) sts. Work even for 7 rows.

Cap Shaping

BO 5 (6, 7) sts at beg of next 2 rows, then decrease 1 st each edge every other row 11 times, every 4 rows 3 times, then every row 7 times—24 (26, 28) sts rem. BO all sts.

Finishing

Block pieces to measurements. With yarn threaded on tapestry needle, sew shoulder seams. Sew sleeves into armholes. Sew side and sleeve seams.

With crochet hook and C, work 1 rnd sc around sleeve hem. Work 1 rnd dc.

RS facing, with crochet hook and B, work sc around outside edges of butterfly motif on both fronts.

Chart A

Chart B

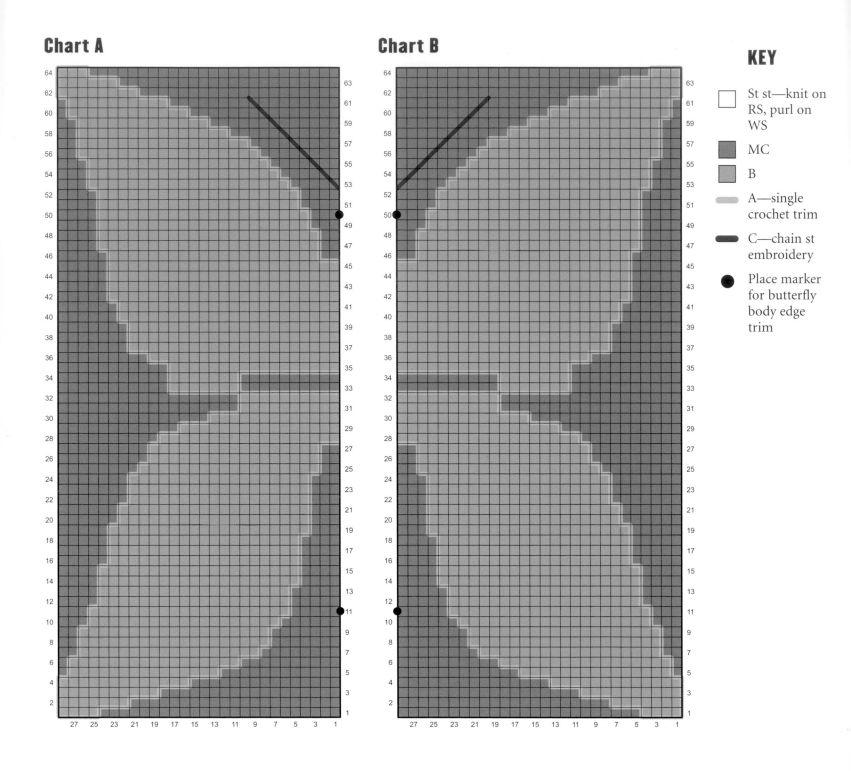

KEY

- ☐ St st—knit on RS, purl on WS
- ■ MC
- ■ B
- ▬ A—single crochet trim
- ▬ C—chain st embroidery
- ● Place marker for butterfly body edge trim

Crochet Trim: With crochet hook and MC, work 1 rnd sc around fronts and back of the sweater as follows:

Beg at left lower marker, work down left front to side seam, across back to right side seam, then up the right front to right lower marker; break yarn, change to B for butterfly body; join MC at right upper marker, work up right front, across back neck, down left front to left upper front marker, break yarn; then change to B for butterfly body.

Work 1 rnd dc, following color changes as est working 3 dc in the right and left front corners.

With C, ch 4 and join into a ring. Work sc in each ch and then each sc until disk is desired size for the butterfly head. Tack head to right front, above butterfly body. With C, work chain st embroidery for antennae on right and left fronts.

Sew hook and eye closure beneath butterfly head. Weave in ends to WS and secure.

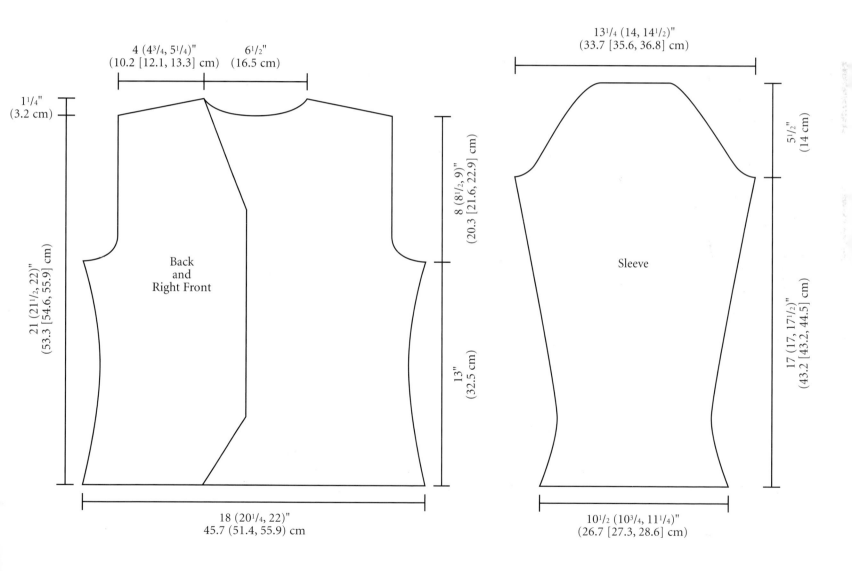

Back and Right Front

4 (4³/₄, 5¹/₄)"
(10.2 [12.1, 13.3] cm)

6¹/₂"
(16.5 cm)

1¹/₄"
(3.2 cm)

21 (21¹/₂, 22)"
(53.3 [54.6, 55.9] cm)

8 (8¹/₂, 9)"
(20.3 [21.6, 22.9] cm)

13"
(32.5 cm)

18 (20¹/₄, 22)"
45.7 (51.4, 55.9) cm

Sleeve

13¹/₄ (14, 14¹/₂)"
(33.7 [35.6, 36.8] cm)

5¹/₂"
(14 cm)

17 (17, 17¹/₂)"
(43.2 [43.2, 44.5] cm)

10¹/₂ (10³/₄, 11¹/₄)"
(26.7 [27.3, 28.6] cm)

Harlequin-Patterned Backpack

For hands-free style, sling this sturdy backpack over your shoulders. Roomy yet low profile, this piece features a clever closure that combines durability with flair. After all, everyday jesters of all stripes can make better use of their hands for juggling shopping bags, hamming it up on their lunch break, and otherwise entertaining at court. (Though you'd be hard pressed to keep this beauty out of the hands of the queen.)

Designer: Lisa B. Evans

Finished Dimensions

Before felting: 30¼" circumference × 13¼" (76.8 cm × 33.7 cm)
After felting: 20½" circumference × 7½" (52.1 cm × 19.1 cm)

Materials
Yarn

Medium, worsted-weight wool

Shown: Rowan Yarns Magpie Aran (100% pure new wool, 153 yards [139.9 m] / 50 g): #688 Teal (A), #686 Tarragon (B), #687 Mexican (C), #685 Coffee Bean (D), #768 Pesto (E), #504 Admiral (F), #684 Berry (G), #778 Harbour (H), 1 hank each

Note: You may also use Nashua Handknits Julia (50% wool, 25% alpaca, 25% kid mohair, 93 yards [85 m] / 50 g), #6396 Deep Blue Sea (A), #5185 Spring Green (B), #0178 Harvest Spice (C), #8118 Espresso (D), #3961 Lady's Mantle (E), #6416 Midnight Blue (F), #6085 Geranium (G), #3983 Delphinium (H), 1 hank each

Needles

One size 8 (5 mm) circular needle, 24" (61 cm) long; set of five size 8 (5 mm) double-pointed needles (dpn)

Notions

Stitch marker; tapestry needle; F/5 (3.75 mm) crochet hook

Gauge

18 sts and 24 rows = 4" (10 cm) in Stockinette st (St st)

Always check your gauge! Adjust needle size to obtain correct gauge if necessary.

Bottom

Note: Change to circular needle when appropriate to fit number of sts. With A and dpn, CO 48 sts. Divide sts evenly among 4 needles as follows: needle 1, 10 sts; needle 2, 4 sts; needle 3, 20 sts; needle 4, 4 sts; needle 1, remaining 10 sts (20 sts total). Join sts into a circle, being careful not to twist CO edge; place marker (pm) for beginning of round (center back). Begin St st.

Shape bottom
Rnd 1, 3, 4, 6, 7, 8, 10, 12, 13, 14, and 16 Knit
Rnd 2 K10, [k1, M1] 4 times, k20, [k1, M1] 4 times, k10—56 sts.
Rnd 5 K10, [k1, M1] 8 times, k20, [k1, M1] 8 times, k10—72 sts.
Rnd 9 K10, [k2, M1] 8 times, k20, [k2, M1] 8 times, k10—88 sts.
Rnd 15 K11, [k1, M1] 22 times, k22, [k1, M1] 22 times, k11—132 sts.
Rnd 17 Knit, increasing 2 sts evenly spaced across row—134 sts.
Rnd 18 Purl (turning row), increasing 2 sts evenly spaced across row—136 sts.

Body

(RS) Working back and forth on circular needle, begin row 1 of chart. Work even through row 66 of chart.

Work eyelet rows as follows:
Row 67 eyelet row 1: K16, [BO last st worked, k12] 3 times, BO last st worked, k32, [BO last st worked, k12] 3 times, BO last st worked, knit to end.
Row 68 eyelet row 2: Work in pattern as est, CO 1 st over BO sts. Work even until all 70 rows of chart are complete. Continuing in A, purl 1 row (turning row). Work even for 2 rows. Repeat eyelet rows 1 and 2.
Work even for 5 rows. BO all sts.

Finishing

Weave in ends to WS and secure. With tapestry needle and A, sew bottom of backpack closed. With tapestry needle and B, sew center back seam, being careful to make chart rows meet at seam. Fold facing to inside at turning row, being careful to make BO holes line up. With tapestry needle and A, sew in place to WS, making sure sts do not show on RS.

Loops (make two): With crochet hook and B, work single-crochet chain 12" (30.5 cm) long. With this chain, work another single-crochet chain approximately 3" (7.6 cm) long. Attach loops to lower back of piece, on each side of center back decorative band.

Strap: With dpn and B, CO 15 sts; divide evenly among 3 needles. Join sts into a circle, being careful not to twist CO edge; place marker (pm) for beginning of round. Work even for 6' (1.8 m). BO all sts. With tapestry needle and B, sew ends of strap closed. Flatten strap and sew running st down both sides to keep it flat and prevent it from rolling during felting.

Flap: With dpn and B, pick up and knit 8 sts to either side of the center back (16 sts total). Begin St st. Work even until piece measures 7" (17.8 cm) from pick-up row, ending with WS row.

To shape flap, decrease 1 st each edge every row 3 times—10 sts rem.

BO 2 sts at beginning of next 2 rows—6 sts rem. BO all sts.

Felting: Place backpack and strap in washing machine with dark towels and/or blue jeans. Follow felting instructions on page 43 When felting is complete, remove backpack and reshape it with your hands, smoothing any folds and molding side pleats. Let backpack and strap air dry.

Cinch Cord: With crochet hook and B, work single-crochet chain 12' (3.7 m) long. With this chain, work another single-crochet chain approximately 40" (101.6 cm) long. Attach center point of cinch cord to top center back of backpack, just below folded edge. Feed cinch cord through eyelet openings, beginning and ending on either side of center front of backpack.

Feed each end of strap beneath cinch cord between center back and first eyelet opening. Then feed strap up through loop at bottom of the backpack; using tapestry needle and B, secure end of strap to itself on WS.

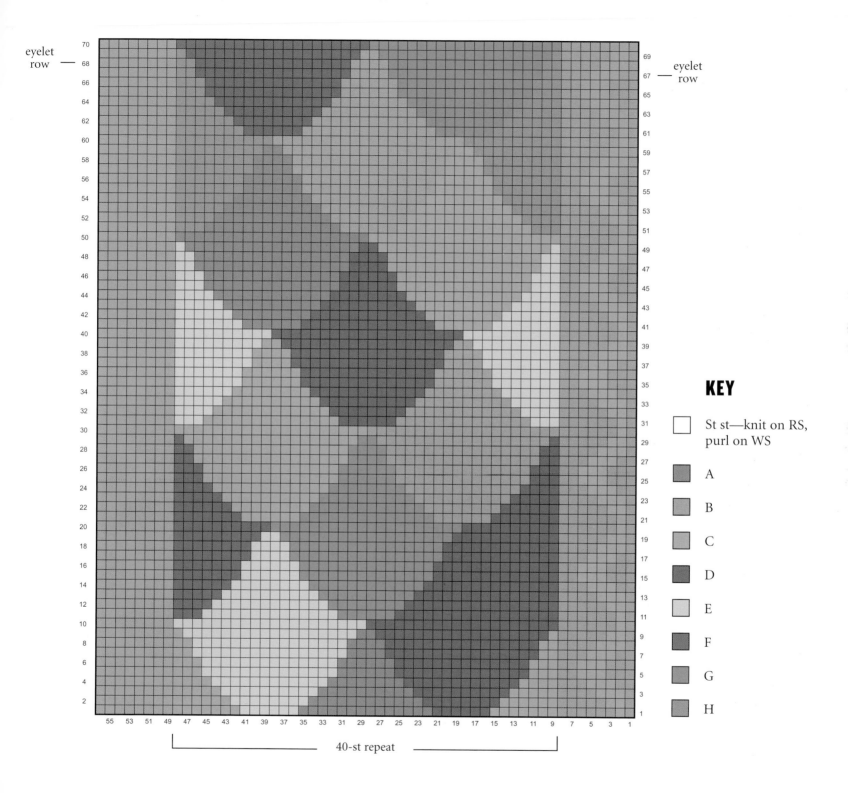

Lily's Bordello Pillow

Tucked away in an alleyway in Dublin is a lush, velvet-draped, sconce-lit club called Lily's Bordello. The club evokes a bygone bohemian era. This pillow is just as suitable on a divan in this bordello, surrounded by Belle Epoque grandeur, as it is on your modern, streamlined couch. (Absinthe not included.)

Designer: Lisa B. Evans

Finished Dimensions

27¼" × 27½" (69.2 × 69.9 cm)

Materials

Yarn

Medium-weight wool blend

Shown: Knit One Crochet Too Parfait Solids (100% wool, 218 yards [199.3 m] / 100 g): #1730 Eggplant (MC), 2 skeins; #1369 Soft Pimento (B) and #1559 Loden (E), 1 skein each

Knit One, Crochet Too Paint Box (100% wool, 100 yards [91.4 m] / 50 g): #05 Blue Spruce (A), #02 Adobe Rose (C), and #03 Spring Moss (D), 1 ball each

Needles

One pair size 8 (5 mm) straight needles, 14" (34.4 cm) long

Notions

Stitch markers; 26" × 26" (66 × 66 cm) pillow form; 1 yard (0.9 m) coordinating fabric backing; loose batting; sewing needle; matching sewing thread

Gauge

16 sts and 21 rows = 4" (10 cm) in Stockinette St (St st)

Always check your gauge! Adjust needle size to obtain correct gauge if necessary.

Pillow Front

With MC, CO 109 stitches. Work even in St st, beg with a knit row, for 20 rows.

Next Row (RS): Beg chart: Work 10 sts, place marker (pm), work across row 1 of chart, pm, work to end. Work even until all 105 rows of chart are complete. Continuing in MC, work even for 20 rows. BO all sts.

Finishing

Steam piece flat. Using pillow front as template, cut fabric backing ½" (1.3 cm) larger on all sides. Lay pillow front on top of fabric backing with right sides together and pin in place. Sew tight seam around 3½ sides of pillow, rounding corners for a smoother look, and leaving an opening of approximately 10" (25.4 cm). Work zigzag st to overcast edges to prevent fraying. Turn pillow cover RS out and insert pillow form. Carefully adjust corners and use loose batting to fill in where desired. Pin remaining opening; sew closed securely with a needle and thread.

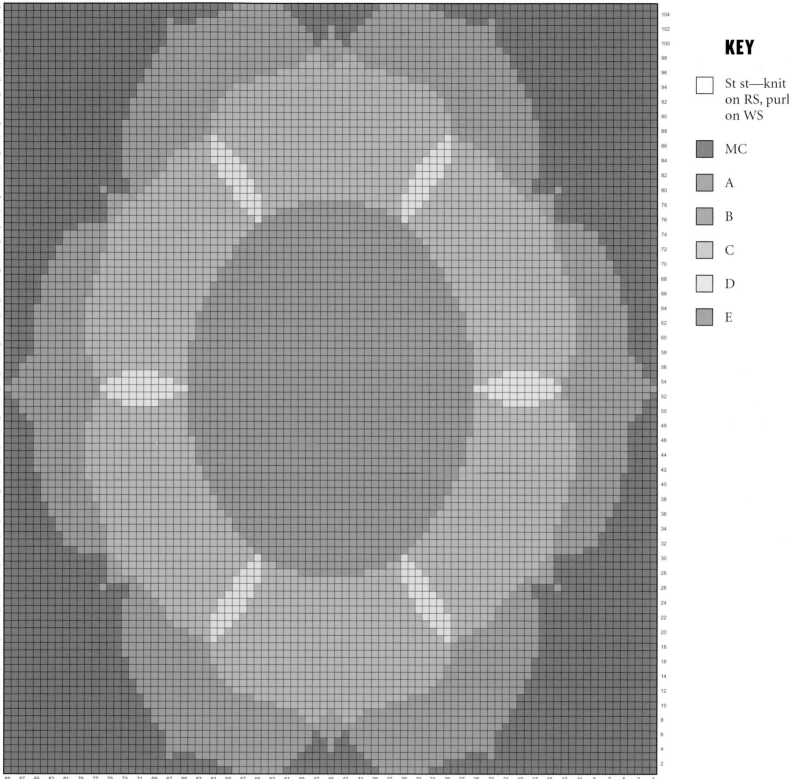

KEY

☐ St st—knit on RS, purl on WS

■ MC

■ A

■ B

■ C

■ D

■ E

Ice Princess
Hair Wrap

This array of cables, bobbles, and textured stitching will keep your ears, and your well-coiffed crown, warm from Milan to Minsk. Change from doubled worsted and chunky weight yarns to a cotton or lightweight blend to "thaw" this icy blue piece into a wrap for warmer climes.

Designer: Rochelle Bourgault

Finished Dimensions

$4^1/_2$" × $30^3/_4$" (11.4 × 78.1 cm), including ties
$4^1/_2$" × $18^3/_4$" (11.4 × 47.6 cm), not including ties

Materials

Yarn

Medium, worsted-weight wool/alpaca blend; chunky-weight wool/alpaca blend

Shown: Nashua Handknits Creative Focus Worsted (75% wool / 25% alpaca, 220 yards [200 m] / 100 g): #2540 Ciel (MC) and #3686 Carolina Blue (A), 1 ball each—2 strands held together throughout

Nashua Handknits Creative Focus Chunky (75% wool / 25% alpaca, 110 yards [100 m] / 100 g): #0100 Natural (B), 1 ball

Needles

One pair size 10 (6 mm) straight needles, 14" (34.4 cm) long

Notions

Cable needle (cn); tapestry needle

Gauge

28 sts and 23 rows = $4^1/_2$" (11.4 cm) over chart

Always check your gauge! Adjust needle size to obtain correct gauge if necessary.

Pattern Stitch
Seed stitch

(multiple of 2 sts).
Row 1 (RS): ✳ K1, p1; repeat from ✳ to end of row.
Row 2 ✳ P1, k1; repeat from ✳ to end of row.
Repeat these 2 rows for pattern.

Design Variations

✳ This warm, wooly head wrap can also be worn around the neck as a cowl or snug collar. If you can't bring yourself to bind off at any logical point, you can also continue knitting until it is as long as a scarf. (You'll have to make sure you have ample yarn for this—double or triple the quantities of the main color and the primary contrasting color. The skein of the secondary contrasting color, the blue that winds its way up the center of the wrap, will last longer.)

Wrap (with Ties)

With two strands of MC, CO 8 sts; begin Seed st. Work even until piece measures 6" (15.2 cm) or desired length from CO edge, ending on a WS row.

Begin row 1 of chart, working increases and changing colors as indicated. Work even until you have completed 5 repeats of rows 9–24 (wrap should measure approximately 17" (43.2 cm) from beg of chart), or to desired length.

Work rows 25–32 of chart, working decreases as indicated—8 sts remain. Continuing in MC, change to Seed st. Work even until piece measures 6" (15.2 cm) or desired length from beg of Seed st, ending on a WS row. BO all sts.

Wrap (without Ties)

With two strands of MC, CO 28 sts. Begin row 9 of chart. Work even until you have completed 5 repeats of rows 9–24 (wrap should measure approximately 15¾" [40 cm] from CO edge), or to desired length, ending on a WS row. BO all sts. With MC threaded on tapestry needle, sew ends together.

Finishing

Weave in ends to WS and secure.

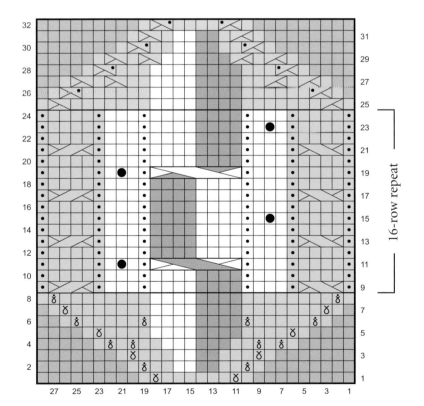

KEY

☐ St st—knit on RS, purl on WS

☐ MC, two strands held together

▨ A, two strands held together

☐ B

▨ No stitch

⊠ M1: make 1 knitwise

⊠ M1-p: make 1 purlwise

• Purl on RS, knit on WS

● MB (make bobble): [K1-f/b, kl-f/b, k1] in same st to inc to 5 sts, turn; p5, turn; pass second, third, fourth, then fifth sts over first st and off needle, k1-tbl

⊠ K2tog

⊠ Ssk

⊠ P2tog

⊠ Ssp

▧ C4F: slip next 2 sts to cn and hold to front of work, k2, k2 from cn

▧ C4B: slip next 2 sts to cn and hold to back of work, k2, k2 from cn

▧ C8F: slip next 4 sts to cn and hold to front of work work, k4, k4 from cn

4

Fair Isle and Stranded Knitting

Fair Isle knitting is a time-honored color knitting technique that comes to us from its namesake in the Shetland Islands, Scotland. Traditionally, this technique consists of only two strands of brilliantly colored wool worked together in a single knitted row. These intricate patterns are built one upon the other, creating the appearance of bands or stripes. Modern designers such as Kaffe Fassett and Alice Starmore have cleverly created beautiful and visually complex designs based upon this classic technique by using large overall patterns and repeating images with subtle and not-so-subtle changes in color.

Unlike intarsia, Fair Isle knitting carries the colors along the back of the knitted piece and may be used in both flat knitting (back and forth) or in the round. Intarsia creates a fabric of a single thickness of knitting, whereas Fair Isle consists of a doubled thickness due to the extra strands being carried behind the work.

This knitting style stands out for its method of carrying color strands. Two methods of carrying are used: stranding and weaving. Stranding is simply carrying one color strand along behind the knitting while working with the other color and switching the working colors every two to three stitches as called for in the design. Weaving is the method of

Cropped Cardigan, page 68

Ella's Argyle Dog Sweater, page 82

carrying the nonworking color for greater distances, such as four to seven stitches, before switching. Both of these methods are used consistently throughout a work as needed from row to row and will become second nature to you in a short period of time. (See illustrated instructions in the Technique Library, page 136, for more on stranding and weaving yarns.)

Tension, or gauge, is the most important consideration with any color knitting technique, and learning to strand or weave will just take a little practice. When working with multiple strands, there are several things that will help you achieve smooth and even knitting. Hold the nonworking strand of yarn lightly while knitting with the working strand. As with knitting in general, keeping your grip light on the needles and yarn makes it much easier to remember not to knit or pull too tightly. Another way to keep your stranding from getting too tight is to spread the knitted stitches out across the needle before changing colors or weaving the strand behind the next stitch. This will ensure that there is ample length to prevent puckering.

Whether stranding or weaving, consistently switching the colors the same way will help prevent the yarn from becoming tangled and unmanageable. Try to always bring color A over the top and color B from below. The result will be fewer yarn tangles and a much neater appearance of your finished piece.

Fair Isle knitting traditionally uses only two colors within a single row, but modern designs may have several more colors working simultaneously. In this case, stranding and weaving as described here can still be used but much more care will need to be taken as the increased number of colors will certainly be more difficult to manage. Yarn management can make or break your enjoyment of a project; even the most simply knitted garments can become a nightmare if the yarns become perpetually tangled and difficult to control.

Cropped Cardigan

This exquisite concoction from knitting luminary Nicky Epstein features traditional Fair Isle patterning with anything but everyday details: sequins, decorative buttons, and an optional fur collar tacked down to the neckband. If you'd prefer to go all-yarn, instructions for a knit collar are included as well.

Designer: Nicky Epstein

Sizes

Small (Medium, Large)
Model shown in size Small.

Finished Dimensions

$36^{1}/_2$ ($40^{1}/_4$, $44^{1}/_4$)" (92.7 [102.2, 112.4] cm), including bands

Materials
Yarn

Medium, worsted-weight wool/alpaca blend

Shown: Nashua Handknits Creative Focus Worsted (75% wool / 25% alpaca, 220 yards [200 m] 100 g): #1460 Juniper (MC), 3 (3, 4) balls; #0202 Camel (A), 2 (2, 3) balls; #0500 Ebony (B), #3317 Mint (C), #4899 Khaki (D), and #1450 Blue Pine (E), 1 (1, 2) balls each

Needles

One size 6 and one size 8 (4 mm and 5 mm) circular needles, 29" (73.7 cm) long; one pair each size 6 and 8 straight needles, 14" (34.4 cm) long

Notions

G/6 (4 mm) crochet hook; stitch holder; six $^{5}/_8$" (1.5 cm) buttons: purchased fur collar (optional); 100 size 11 seed beads to match; 100 5 mm iridescent clear sequins; sewing needle and thread to match beads or fur collar

Gauge

26 sts and 26 rows = 4" (10 cm) over Fair Isle pattern with larger needles

Pattern Stitches
Caliper Cables

(multiple of 13 sts + 3)

Rows 1 and 3 (WS): K3, ✲ [p1, wrapping yarn twice], p8, [p1, wrapping yarn twice], k3; rep from ✲ to end of row.

Rows 2 and 4 P3, *drop next st and extra wrap, k4, pick up and knit dropped st, sl 4 sts purlwise wyib, drop next st and extra wrap, sl 4 sts back to left-hand needle, pick up and knit dropped st, k4, p3; rep from ✲ to end of row.

Row 5 K3, *p10, k3; rep from ✲ to end of row.

Row 6 P3, *k10, p3; rep from ✲ to end of row.

Rep rows 1–6 for the pattern.

Caliper Cables for Buttonhole Band (with buttonholes)

Rows 1 and 3 (WS): K3, [p1, wrapping yarn twice], p8, [p1, wrapping yarn twice], k1.

Rows 2 and 4 P1, drop next st and extra wrap, k4, pick up and knit dropped st, sl 4 sts purlwise wyib, drop next st and extra wrap, sl 4 sts back to left-hand needle, pick up and knit dropped st, k4, p3.

Row 5 K3, p4, BO next 2 sts, p4, k1.

Row 6 P3, ✲ k4, CO 2 sts, k4, p1.

✲

Notes This sweater is worked in one piece, then divided for the armholes. You may work a single crochet neck edge, as shown above, or the optional caliper cables neckband. Here, vintage wooden buttons were used; artisan glass buttons are shown with the fur collar option on page 69.

Caliper Cables for Buttonhole Band (without buttonholes)

Rows 1 and 3 (WS): K3, [p1, wrapping yarn twice], p8, [p1, wrapping yarn twice], k1.

Rows 2 and 4 P1, drop next st and extra wrap, k4, pick up and knit dropped st, sl 4 wyib, drop next st and extra wrap, sl 4 sts back to left-hand needle, pick up and knit dropped st, k4, p3.

Row 5 K3, p10, k1.

Row 6 P3, k10, p1.

1x1 Rib

(multiple of 2 sts + 1)

Row 1 ✳ K1, p1; rep from ✳ to last st, k1.

Row 2 ✳ P1, k1; rep from ✳ to last st, p1.

Rep Rows 1–2 for pattern.

Body

With size 6 circular needle, CO 224 (250, 276) sts. Beg caliper cables. Work even until piece measures 4½ (5½, 6½)" (11.4 [14, 16.5] cm) from CO edge, ending with row 6 of pattern.

(WS) Change to size 8 needle and St st, beg with a purl row, inc 0 (2, 2) sts evenly spaced across first row—224 (248, 274) sts.

(RS) Beg chart A as indicated for your size. Work even until entire chart is complete. Following chart sequence (see Chart Notes, next page), work even until the piece measures 10" (25.4 cm) from CO edge, ending on a WS row.

Divide for Armholes

Right front: (RS) Work across 53 (59, 65) sts; place rem 171 (189, 209) sts on holder for back and left front. Continuing in pattern and chart sequence as est, working back and forth on right front, work even until piece measures 15" (35.6 cm) from CO edge, ending on a WS row.

Shape neckline: (RS) BO 12 sts at beg of next RS row, 3 sts at beg of next RS row, 2 sts at beg of next 2 (2, 1) RS rows, then dec 1 st at neck edge every other row 4 (4, 5) times—30 (36, 43) sts rem. Work even until chart sequence has been completed (piece should measure approximately 17½ (18½, 19½)" (44.5 [47, 49.5] cm) from CO edge). BO all sts.

Back: (RS) Rejoin yarn to sts on holder. Continuing in pattern and chart sequence as est, work across 118 (130, 144) sts for back; place rem 53 (59, 65) sts on holder for left front. Work even until chart sequence has been completed. BO all sts.

Left front: (RS) Rejoin yarn to sts on holder. Complete as for right front, reversing all shaping.

Sleeves (make two)

Using size 6 straight needles, CO 55 sts. Beg caliper cables. Work even for 7 rows, ending on a WS row.

Shape sleeve

(RS) Inc 1 st each edge every other row 6 times, working inc sts in St st as they become available (you should have completed row 6 of caliper cables)—67 sts.

(WS) Change to size 8 straight needles; St st and purl 1 row.

(RS) Beg chart sequence (see Chart Notes, page 72) and, at the same time, inc 1 st each edge every other row 2 (8, 14) times, then every 4 rows 20 (17, 14) times, working inc sts in pattern as they become available—111 (117, 123) sts. Work even until piece measures 18" (45.7 cm) or desired length from CO edge. BO all sts.

Finishing

Block pieces to measurements. Sew shoulders. Sew in sleeves. Sew sleeve seams.

Buttonhole Band: With size 6 straight needles and MC, CO 14 sts. Beg caliper cables for buttonhole band. ✳ Work rows 1–6 with buttonholes once. Work rows 1–6 without buttonholes twice. Rep from ✳ 4 times. Work Rows 1–6 with buttonholes once. BO all sts. With MC threaded on tapestry needle, sew band to right front.

Chart Notes

Work the following chart sequence: A, B, C, D. Repeat the sequence in reverse order, working from the top to the bottom of each chart, and beginning with row 8 of chart D (do not repeat row 9 of chart D).

When working the sleeves, follow the same chart sequence as for the body. The beginning st will be given for the first time each chart is worked. When the chart is worked again in reverse sequence, be sure to line the chart up over its earlier occurrence. (Note: If you choose not to follow the sleeve shaping as given, you may line the charts up over the center st shown in each chart, then work back to the edge to determine what st to begin on.)

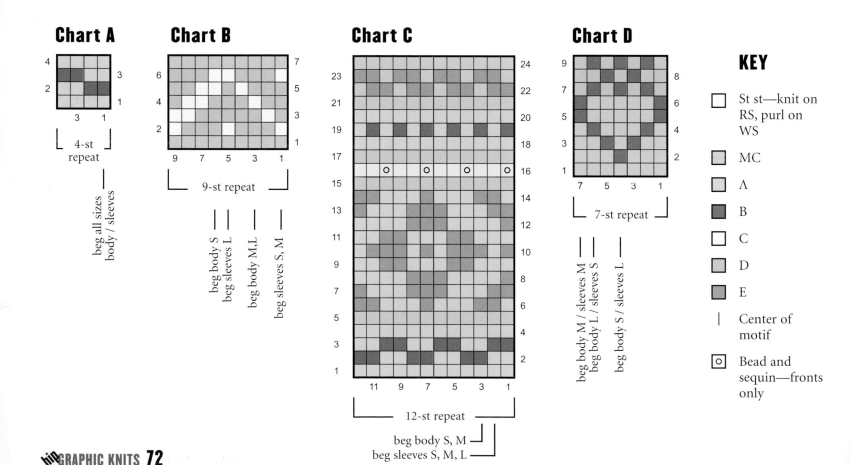

Chart A · **Chart B** · **Chart C** · **Chart D** · **KEY**

KEY
- ☐ St st—knit on RS, purl on WS
- MC
- A
- B
- C
- D
- E
- | Center of motif
- ⊡ Bead and sequin—fronts only

Button Band: With size 6 straight needles and MC, CO 9 sts. Beg 1x1 Rib. Work even until piece measures same as front to beg of neck shaping when slightly stretched. BO all sts in pattern. With MC threaded on tapestry needle, sew to left front. Sew buttons on opposite buttonholes. Weave in ends to WS and secure.

Neckband: RS facing, with crochet hook and MC, beg at right front neck edge, work 1 rnd sc around entire neckline. Fasten off.

Fur Collar (optional): Line up the center of the purchased fur collar with the center back of neckband of the cardigan. Pin the fur collar in place with straight pins. With a hand sewing needle and matching thread, tack down the fur collar to the knit edge of the cardigan, anchoring the thread with small knots in regular intervals. Fasten off thread and trim ends.

Caliper Cables Neckband (optional, worked instead of single crochet): RS facing, with straight needles and MC, beg at right front neck edge, pick up and knit 120 sts evenly around neckline. Beg caliper cables. Work even until neckband measures approximately 1½" (3.8 cm) from pick-up row, ending on row 6 of pattern. BO all sts.

Beads: With sewing needle and thread, sew beads and sequins to fronts of sweater only, as indicated in chart D and as follows:

Bring thread up from WS, through sequin, then through bead. Take thread over outside edge of bead, then back through sequin to WS. Fasten off and secure tail.

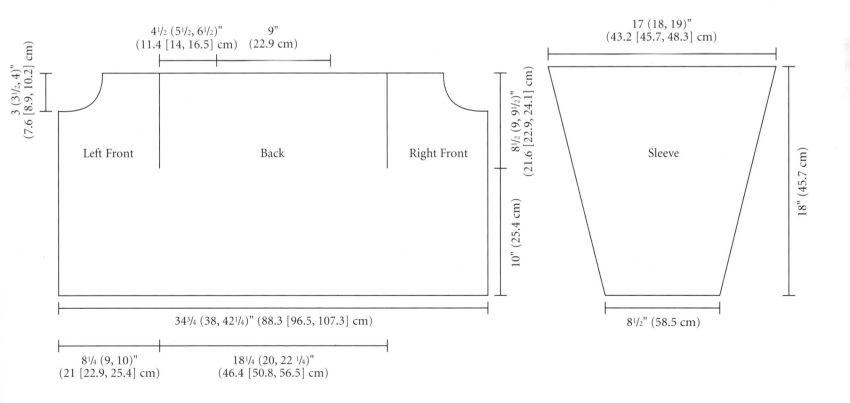

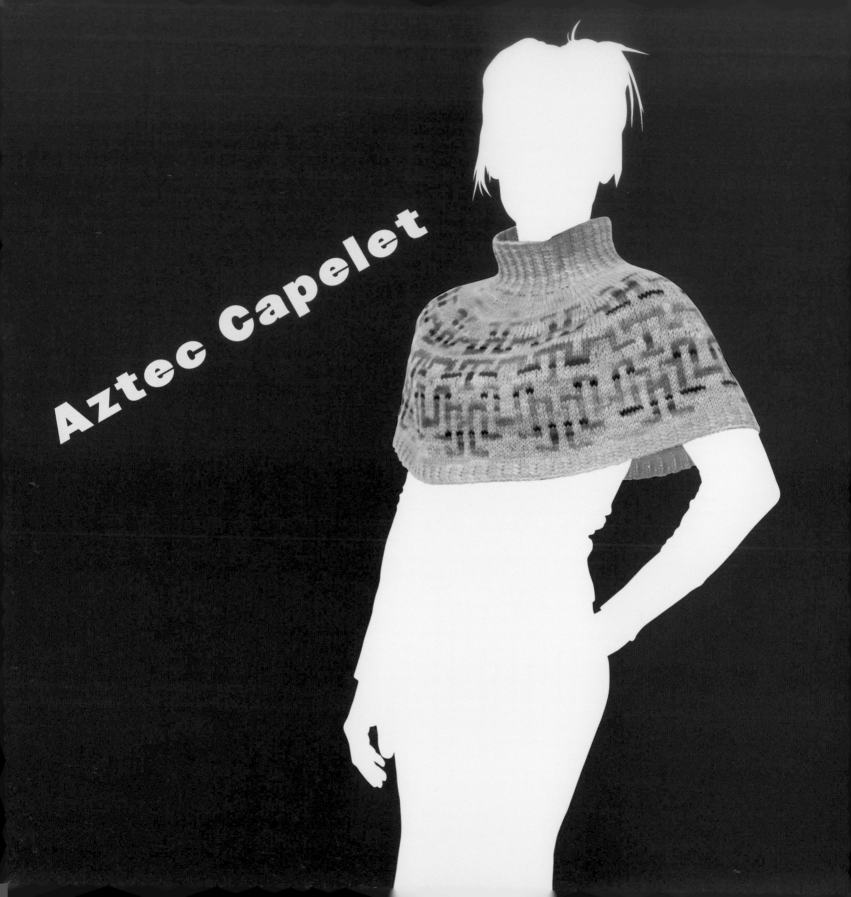

Aztec Capelet

A capelet is a sleek alternative to a wrap, and completes any casual ensemble with panache. The repeated motif has a graduated, triangular shape, designed to accommodate and enhance the bell shaping of the piece.

Designer: Mercedes Tarasovich-Clark

Sizes

Small (Medium, Large)
Model shown in size Small.

Finished Dimensions

46½ (52, 56 ¾)" (118.1 [132.1, 144.1] cm) bottom circumference

Materials

Yarn

Medium, worsted-weight wool

Shown: Araucania Nature Wool Worsted (100% wool, 240 yards [219.5 m]/100 g): #37 Apricot (MC), 1 (2, 2) skeins; #03 Aqua (CC), #27 Green (CC), #07 Teal (CC), and #19 chocolate (CC), 1 skein each

Needles

Size 5 (3.75 mm) circular needles, 29" (73.7 cm) and 16" (40.6 cm) long; size 7 (4.5 mm) circular needle, 29" (73.7 cm); size 7 circular needle, 24" (61 cm) long (optional)

Notions

Stitch marker

Gauge

21 sts and 19½ rows = 4" (10 cm) in Stockinette st (St st), after blocking

Always check your gauge! Adjust needle size to obtain correct gauge if necessary.

Pattern Stitch
Mini-cable Rib
(multiple of 4 sts)

T2F (twist 2 front): With right-hand needle, skip first st on left-hand needle and knit next st through back loop. Leave st on needle. Knit first st on left-hand needle through front loop. Slip both stitches from needle.

Setup Rnd: * K2, p2; repeat from * to end of rnd.

Rnd 1 Rnd 1: repeat setup rnd.

Rnd 2 Rnd 2: * T2F, p2; repeat from * to end of rnd.

Repeat rnds 1 and 2 for the pattern.

Notes The chart is written for MC and one CC. The model was worked in randomly placed stripes of the four contrasting colors. Use one single CC, or work in as many colors as you please, changing colors to suit your taste.

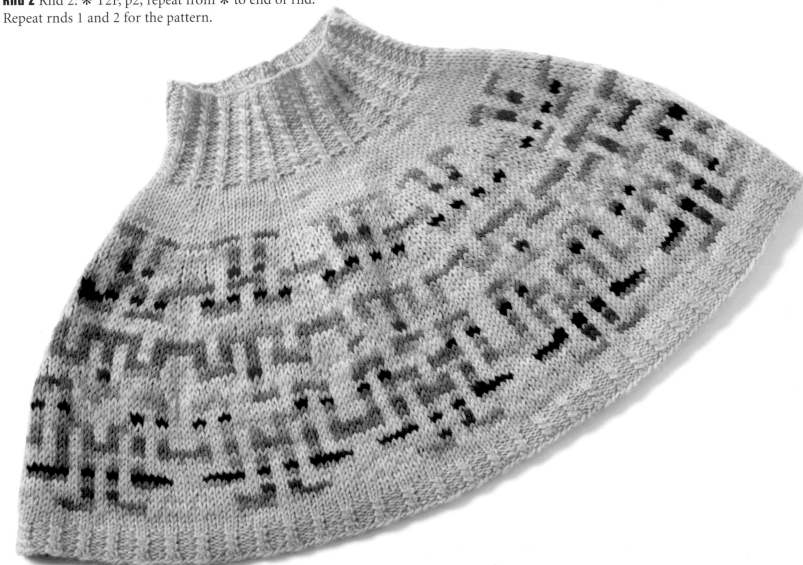

Capelet

Note: Change to shorter circular needle as appropriate for number of sts on needle.

With MC and size 5, 29" (73.7 cm) circular needle, CO 232 (260, 284) sts. Join sts into a circle, being careful not to twist CO edge; place marker (pm) for beginning of round.

Beg mini-cable rib. Work even until piece measures 1" (2.5 cm) from CO edge. Change to size 7, 29" (73.7 cm) circular needle and St st, increase 2 (0, 2) sts evenly spaced around—234 (260, 286) sts. Work even for 3 rnds.

Begin row 1 of chart, working decreases as indicated, and changing contrasting colors as desired—90 (100, 110) sts remain. Change to size 5, 16" (40.6 cm) circular needle and mini-cable rib. Work even until piece measures 3½ (4, 4½)" (8.9 [10.2, 11.4] cm) from beg of mini-cable rib. BO all sts loosely in pattern.

Finishing

Weave in all ends to WS and secure. Block piece to measurements.

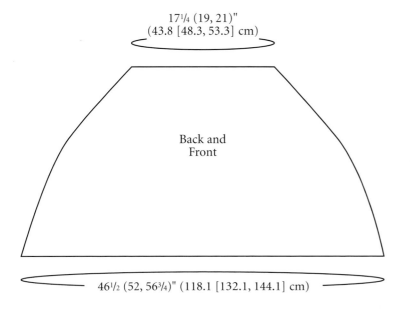

17¼ (19, 21)"
(43.8 [48.3, 53.3] cm)

Back and Front

46½ (52, 56¾)" (118.1 [132.1, 144.1] cm)

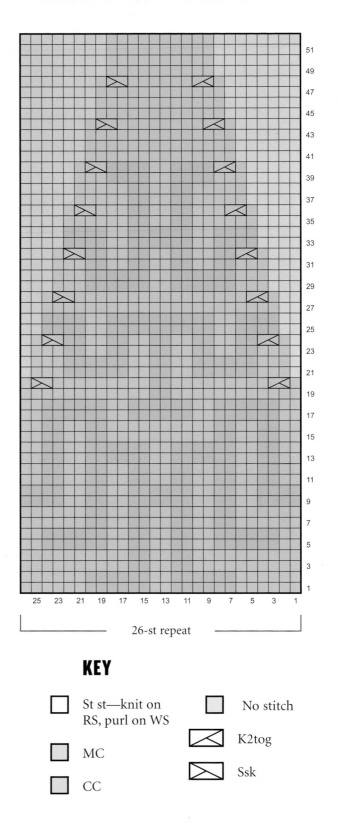

26-st repeat

KEY

☐ St st—knit on RS, purl on WS	☐ No stitch
☐ MC	⊠ K2tog
☐ CC	⊠ Ssk

Meanwhile, Back at the Ranch Belt

Suitable for any gunslinging cowgirl, this belt can be paired with a simple sheath dress or well-worn jeans and a white T-shirt. Finish it off with a showpiece silver buckle, as shown, or paw through your stash (or the stock of your local craft store) for a buckle that suits your wardrobe.

Designer: Mercedes Tarasovich-Clark

Finished Dimensions

3.5" × 44" (8.9 × 111.8 cm) including crochet edging
Shown in size Medium.

Materials

Yarn

Medium, aran-weight nylon

Shown: Berroco Suede Tri-Color (100% nylon, 120 yds (109.7 m) / 50 g), #3797 Django (MC), 2 balls

Berroco Suede (100% nylon, 120 yds (109.7 m) / 50 g), #3789 Nelly Belle (A), #3768 Sundance Kid (B), #3719, Texas Rose (C), 1 ball each

Needles

One pair size 5 (3.75 mm) straight needles, 1 pair, 14" (34.4 cm) long

Gauge

22 sts and 30 rows = 4" (10 cm) in Stockinette st (St st).

Always check your gauge! Adjust needle size to obtain correct gauge if necessary.

Notions

G/6 (4 mm) crochet hook, ⅛ to ¼ yard (0.1 to 0.2 m) sueded rayon fabric for backing; 1 to 1½ yards (0.9 to 1.4 m) 3" (7.6 cm) -wide buckram or heavy-duty interfacing for liner; sewing needles; matching sewing thread; hook closure belt buckle; awl (optional).

Notes The chart does not need to be followed exactly as given. Always keep the background in MC as shown, but feel free to mix and match the contrasting colors and motifs to suit your taste.

You may choose between a buckle closure and an optional fringe tie closure. Instructions for both are given.

Design Variations

✳ More of an urban cowgirl? Lose the brown suede backing and edging detail and opt for black pleather or any au courant fabric of choice. Any kind of fabric that offers sturdiness is a good choice.

Belt

With MC, CO 10 sts. Beg St st, slipping first st of each row purlwise. Work even until piece measures 1½" (3.8cm) from CO edge, ending on WS row. Continuing in St st, inc 1 st at beg of row every row 8 times—18 sts. Work even for 2 rows. Beg Row 1 of Chart. Work even until piece measures 7" (17.8cm) less than desired belt circumference. Continuing in MC, work even for 2 rows. Dec 1 st at beg of row every row 8 times—10 sts rem.

Buckle Closure:

Work even for 7½" (19.1 cm) or to desired strap length. Dec 1 st at beg of each row 6 times—4 sts rem. BO rem sts.

Fringe Tie Closure (optional):

Work even for 1½" (3.8 cm). BO all sts.

Finishing

Weave in ends to WS and secure.

Crochet Edging: RS facing, with crochet hook and MC, work reverse single crochet along edge sts. Fasten off. Block lightly.

Lining: Cut buckram to fit length and width of Belt, less ¼" (6 mm) on each edge, so that liner will fit just within crocheted edge. Using the buckram as a template, cut fabric, leaving ¼" (6 mm) seam allowance on all sides. Layer buckram between belt and fabric, turning fabric seam allowance under; pin in place. Sew fabric and buckram in place.

Buckle Closure: Sew buckle in place on short end of Belt. The buckle hook can be hooked into the surface of the knit fabric, or for reinforced belt notches, use a sharp awl to pierce through all three fabric layers in desired spot, then reinforce hole with sewing thread.

Fringe Tie Closure: Cut thirty 14" (35.6 cm) lengths of MC yarn. With crochet hook and 3 strands for each Fringe, work Fringe at 5 points along each end of Belt.

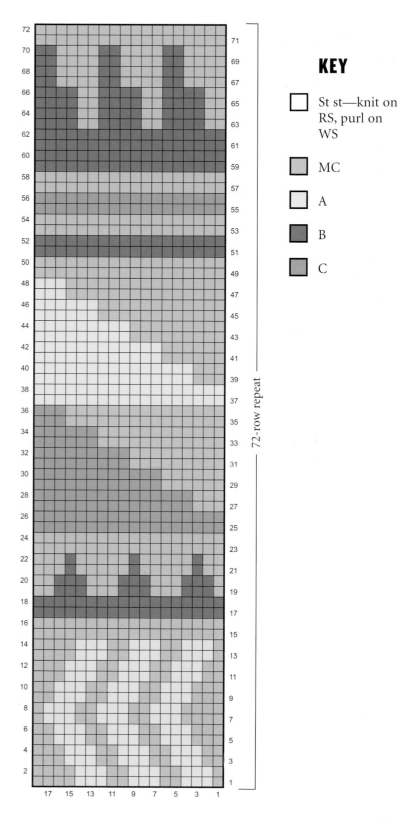

KEY

☐	St st—knit on RS, purl on WS
☐	MC
☐	A
☐	B
☐	C

72-row repeat

Ella's Argyle Dog Sweater

What better way to assert your exquisite sense of hipster style than by getting your canine companion in on the deal? If your pup could talk, she'd likely beg for a wardrobe upgrade before she begged for bacon or beef. (You'd get bored with the same old year-round coat, too!) This classic argyle, however unorthodox its use, will take any dog to new heights of fashion. (See page 86 for a coordinating pair of "people" mittens.)

Designer: Cecelia Wu

Sizes

Small (Medium, Large)
Model shown in size Small.

Finished Dimensions

14¼ (18¼, 22)" (36.2 [46.4, 55.9] cm) circumference × 10 (14, 20)" (25.4 [35.6, 50.8] cm) long

Materials
Yarn

Medium-weight merino wool

Shown: Patons Classic Merino Wool (100% wool, 223 yds [225 m] / 100 g): #00212 Royal Purple (MC), #00218 Peacock (A), #00240 Leaf Green (B), #77732 That's Pink (C), 1 ball each

Needles

One pair size 7 (4.5 mm) straight needles, 14" (34.4 cm) long

Notions

Stitch markers; tapestry needle

Gauge

15 sts and 16 rows = 4" (10 cm) in Stockinette st (St st)

Always check your gauge! Adjust needle size to obtain correct gauge if necessary.

Pattern stitch
2 x 2 Rib

(multiple of 4 sts + 2)
Row 1 (RS): K2, ✳ p2, k2; repeat from ✳ to end of row.
Row 2 P2, ✳ k2, p2; repeat from ✳ to end of Row.
Repeat Rows 1–2 for pattern.

Back

With MC, CO 38 (50, 58) sts. Beg 2 × 2 Rib. Work even for 4 (6, 8) rows, inc 3 (1, 3) sts evenly spaced on last row—41 (51, 61) sts. (RS) Beg Row 1 of Chart A. Work even for 21 (31, 51) rows (piece should measure approximately 6¼ (9, 14)" (15.9 [22.9, 35.6] cm) from CO edge. Change to MC and St st, beg with a purl row, dec 6 sts evenly spaced across first row—35 (45, 55) sts rem.

Shape back

Continuing in St st, BO 3 sts at beg of next 2 rows—29 (39, 49) sts rem.

Sizes Medium and Large Only: BO 2 sts at beg of next 2 rows—35 (45) sts rem.

Size Large Only: BO 1 st at beg of next 2 rows—43 sts rem.

All Sizes: Change to 2 × 2 Rib, dec 3 (1, 1) sts evenly spaced on first row—26 (34, 42) sts rem. Work even until piece measures 10 (14, 20)" (25.4 [35.6, 50.8] cm) or desired length from CO edge. BO all sts in pattern.

Chart A

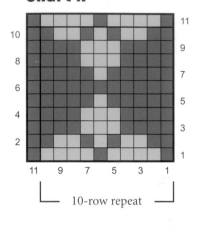

10-row repeat

KEY

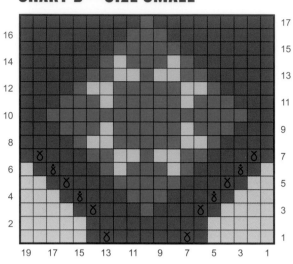

☐ St st—knit on RS, purl on WS

☐ MC

☐ A

☐ B

☐ C

☐ No stitch

⑧ M1: Make 1 knitwise

⑧ M1-p: Make 1 purlwise

CHART B—SIZE SMALL

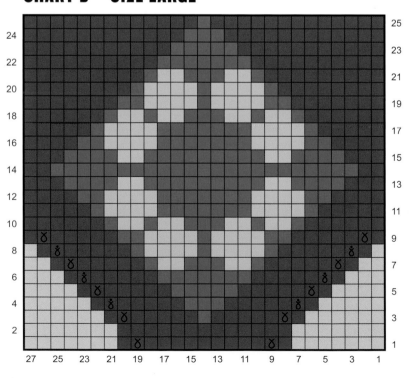

CHART C—SIZE MEDIUM

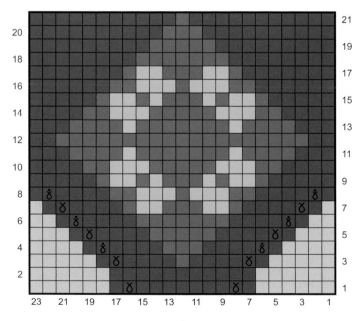

CHART D—SIZE LARGE

Front

With MC, CO 7 (9, 11) sts. Beg Row 1 of Chart B (C, D), working incs as indicated. Work even until entire Chart is complete—19 (23, 27) sts. Continuing in MC, work even until piece measures 6¾ (10, 15½)" (17.1 [25.4, 39.4] cm) from CO edge, ending on a WS row, inc 3 sts evenly spaced across last row—22 (26, 30) sts. Change to 2 × 2 Rib. Work even until piece measures 8½ (12, 17½)" (21.6 [30.5, 44.5] cm) or desired length from CO edge. BO all sts in pattern.

Finishing

Weave in ends to WS and secure. Block pieces to measurements. Place markers 1½ (2, 2½)" (3.8 [5.1, 6.4] cm) and 4½ (5½, 6½)" (11.4 [14, 16.5] cm) down from CO edge along each side of back and front, to mark beg and end of leg opening. Sew from CO edge to first marker. Cut yarn. Sew from second marker to end of front. (Note: To make adjustments to leg holes for proper fit, try sweater on dog after sewing to first marker. Place second marker for end of leg opening; sew from second marker to end of front.)

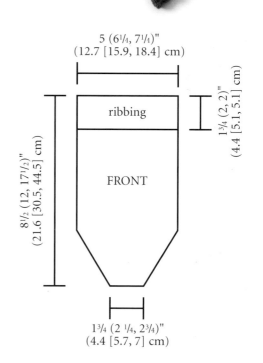

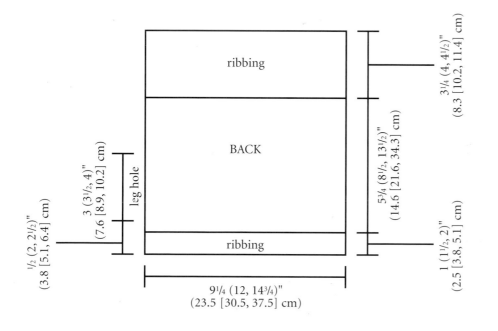

Looking for a cozy way to ride your canine's coattails? These mittens feature a stranded argyle band, knit in the round, designed to coordinate with Ella's Argyle Dog Sweater (see page 82). Argyles are the equal-opportunity motifs of the design world—they work well in many color combinations, proportions, and sizes. If you're sheepish about coordinating with your pooch, choose a color that suits *you* to a T.

Designer: Rochelle Bourgault

Finished Dimensions

Circumference: 8³/₄" (22.2 cm)
Length: 8¹/₂" (21.6 cm)—see pattern for adjusting length

Materials

Yarn

Medium-weight merino wool

Shown: Patons Classic Merino Wool (100% wool, 223 yards [225 m] / 100 g): #00212 Royal Purple (MC), #00240 Leaf Green (A), #00218 Peacock (B), #77732 That's Pink (C), 1 ball each (or use leftover yarn Ella's Argyle Dog Sweater, page 82)

Needles

Five size 5 and 6 (3.75 mm and 4 mm) double-pointed needles (dpn)

Notions

Stitch markers; stitch holder; tapestry needle

Gauge

18 sts and 27 rows = 4" (10 cm) in Stockinette st (St st) with larger needles

Always check your gauge! Adjust needle size to obtain correct gauge if necessary.

Pattern Stitch
2 x 2 Rib in the Round
(multiple of 4 sts)

All Rnds: ✳ K2, p2; rep from ✳ to end of rnd

Mittens (make 2)
With smaller needles and MC, CO 44 sts. Divide sts onto 4 needles (11 sts each). Join work into a circle, being careful not to twist sts. Place marker (pm) at beg of rnd.

Cuff
Begin 2 × 2 Rib. Work even until piece measures 2" (5.1 cm) or desired length from CO edge.

Mitten Body
Change to larger needles. Dec 4 sts across first rnd as follows:

First needle: K2tog, knit to end of needle. Second needle: Knit to last 2 sts, ssk. Third needle: K2tog, knit to end of needle. Fourth needle: Knit to last 2 sts, ssk—40 sts rem.

Thumb
K19, pm, M1-R, k2, m1-L, pm, knit to end of rnd—42 sts. Knit 1 rnd. Inc 2 sts next rnd, every 3 rnds 3 times, then every other rnd once, as follows:

Knit to marker, slip marker (sm), M1-R, knit to next marker, m1-L, sm, knit to end—52 sts.

Mitten Body (continued)

K20, place next 12 sts on holder for thumb, CO 4 sts for bottom of thumb gusset, knit to end of rnd—44 sts. Redistribute sts evenly among needles. Work even on these sts for 4 rnds. Beg argyle motif from chart. Work even until entire chart is complete. Continuing in MC, work even for 6 rnds, or until hand portion of mitten reaches tip of your pinkie.

Fingertip Decreases

Decrease 4 sts this rnd, every other rnd twice, then every rnd 3 times, as follows:

On each needle, knit to last 2 sts on needle, k2tog—20 sts rem. Next rnd, ✱ K2tog; rep from ✱ around—10 sts rem.

Finishing

Cut yarn, leaving 8" (20.3 cm) tail. Thread tapestry needle with tail and weave through rem stitches, pulling firmly to close. Weave in ends to WS and secure.

Thumb: Divide sts from thumb holder onto 3 larger needles; using MC, pick up and knit 4 sts from bottom of thumb gusset—16 sts. Beg St st. Work even until piece measures 2" (5.1 cm) or to tip of your thumb from pickup rnd.

Thumb Tip Decreases: Decrease 4 sts this rnd, then every other rnd once, as follows:

On each needle, k2tog, knit to end of needle—8 sts rem.

Next rnd: ✱ K2tog; rep from ✱ to end of rnd—4 sts rem. Cut yarn, leaving 8" (20.3 cm) tail. Thread tapestry needle with tail and weave through rem stitches, pulling firmly to close. Weave in ends to WS and secure.

Design Variation

In this pattern, the mittens are identical, and it makes no difference where the thumb is oriented— the Fair Isle colorwork appears around the entire mitten. If you prefer to have the motif on the back of your hand only, look to the Baby, What's Your Sign? Socks (see page 114) for guidance on how to divide the pattern and apply your own design style. With the method outlined in that pattern, you simply need to be vigilant as to how the thumb is oriented: to the left or to the right of the knit motif.

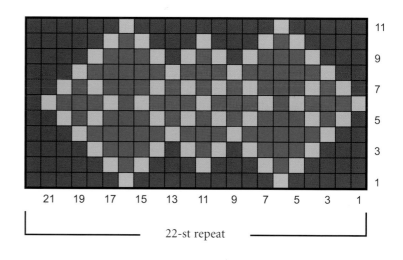

22-st repeat

KEY

☐ St st—knit on RS, purl on WS

☐ A

■ MC

■ B

■ C

Pear Amour
Leg Warmers

It's a visual pun and wordplay feeding frenzy when you wear these pieces. The pear and heart motif employs traditional two-color Fair Isle patterning while upping the style ante by applying it to boot-cut leg warmers. (Yes, the '80s may be far behind us, but leg warmers are back—don't let anyone convince you otherwise.)

Designer: Rochelle Bourgault

Finished Dimensions
18" × 14 ½" (45.7 × 36.8 cm)

Materials
Yarn
Light-weight wool/cotton blend

Shown: Rowan Wool Cotton (50% merino wool / 50% cotton, 123 yards [113 m]/ 50 g): #943 Flower (MC), 6 balls #901 Citron (A), 2 balls

Rowan Cotton Glace (100% cotton, 137 yards [115 m] / 50 g): #816 Mocha Choc (B), 1 ball

Needles
One pair size 7 (4.5 mm) straight needles, 14" (34.4 cm) long; one pair size 8 (5 mm) straight needles, 14" (34.4 cm) long

Notions
Tapestry needle

Gauge
20 sts and 26 rows = 4" (10 cm) in Stockinette st (St st) with 2 strands of yarn held together

Always check your gauge! Adjust needle size to obtain correct gauge if necessary.

Is Doubling Up Yarn "Cheating"?

Choosing to double up yarn to knit a project quicker might make some purists cringe. Enormous needles and a strand of yarn whose diameter approaches that of a garter snake might feel like cheating to those who have a reverence for fine hand-craft and the art of this precise, time-consuming labor of love. However, if doubling, or even tripling, a chosen yarn will result in the desired effect without compromising the integrity of the resulting fabric or garment, there is no reason not to do just that. The Ice Princess Hair Wrap (page 62), Pear Amour Leg Warmers (page 90), Eve's Garden Cover-up Coat (page 98) and Peruvian Lovebird Hat (page 110) all feature doubled, tripled, or even quadrupled yarn. In each of these designs, the chosen yarn was doubled in order to attain a desired fiber content and color palette, practical gauge, or overall look.

A fabric created with doubled wool will create a denser, heartier felt. Two strands of different yarns (a ribbon yarn with a Tencel cotton, for example) will result in a motley, tweedy hybrid. Doubling four-ply tweed for a knee-skimming cardigan will halve the knitting time without losing the refined style. When tinkering with yarns, always take the time to check gauge to ensure your sizing will be accurate—and go with it.

Besides, the dyed-in-the-wool purists are rarely keeping watch over the rest of us.

Notes Leg warmers are worn with ribbing just beneath the knee; the rolled bound-off edge creates a boot-cut legging style, and is perfect with heels.

Leg Warmer (Make Two)

With size 7 needles and 2 strands of MC held together, CO 60 sts. Beg 2 × 2 Rib; work even until piece measures 4" (10.2 cm) from CO edge, ending on WS row.

Change to size 8 needles and St st, increase 1 st each edge every other row 6 times—72 stitches. Work even until piece measures 10" (25.4 cm) from CO edge, ending on WS row.

Beg Pear Amour motif from chart, using Fair Isle (stranded) technique (see page 136). Work all 42 rows of chart. Change to MC and work even in St st for 6 rows. BO all sts knitwise.

Finishing

Weave in ends to WS and secure. Block pieces to measurements. Sew side seams.

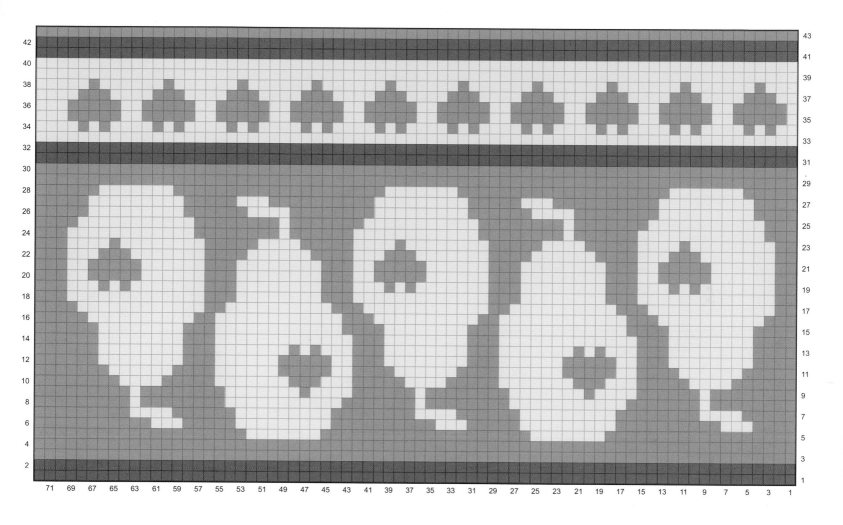

KEY

☐ St st—knit on RS, purl on WS

▨ MC

☐ A

▨ B

Tribal Sun
Messenger Bag

Too squeamish for a tattoo? Looking for something just as edgy but a little less permanent? Emblazon a crisp, tattoo-inspired motif across the front flap of this messenger bag: no painful procedures required. This project is lined for added durability; as constructed, the lining doubles as a piping detail, peeking out from the seams.

Designer: Lisa B. Evans

Finished Dimensions

10½" × 9½" × 2¾" (26.7 × 24.1 × 7 cm)

Materials
Yarn

Medium-weight cotton/acrylic blend

Shown: Nashua Handknits Cilantro (70% cotton / 30% acrylic, 136 yards [124.4 m] / 50 g): #001 Delft Blue (MC), 4 balls; #013 Marine (A), 1 ball

Needles

One pair size 8 (5 mm) straight needles, 14" (34.4 cm) long

Notions

Lining fabric, approx ¾ yard (0.7 m); sewing needle; matching sewing thread

Gauge

20 sts and 30 rows = 4" (10 cm) in Stockinette st (St st)

Always check your gauge! Adjust needle size to obtain correct gauge if necessary.

Pattern Stitch
Seed Stitch

(multiple of 2 sts)
Row 1 (RS): ✳ K1, p1; repeat from ✳ to end of row
Row 2 ✳ P1, k1; repeat from ✳ to end of row
Repeat these 2 rows for pattern.

Body

With MC, CO 56 sts. Purl 1 row. (RS) Beg row 1 of the chart.
Work even until entire chart is complete (piece should measure
approximately 8" [20.3 cm] from CO edge).

Work even until piece measures 30" (76.2 cm) from CO edge,
ending on WS row. BO all sts.

Strap

With MC, CO 30 sts. Beg Seed st. Work even until piece
measures 45" (114.3 cm) or 60" (152.4 cm) for a low-
slung look. BO all stitches. Fold strap in half width-
wise and sew basting stitch along both long edges to
hold it in place.

Finishing

Block body of bag to measure approximately
11" × 30" (27.9 × 76.2 cm). Lay body face
down on lining fabric and pin it in place
at close intervals to assure that edges
are straight. Trim fabric to fit body;
sew it firmly in place, leaving
approximately 4" (10.7 cm) open at
end opposite motif. Turn RS out,
being careful to fully turn corners;
pin opening and sew it closed.

Assembly

Note: Seams are sewn to the outside, exposing the lining fabric
as a colorful accent.

Beg at end opposite motif lay body knit-side down and align 8"
(20.3 cm) of strap ends with center 8" (20.3 cm) of body with
folded edge to front of bag. Pin it in
place, leaving small amount
of lining fabric
exposed.

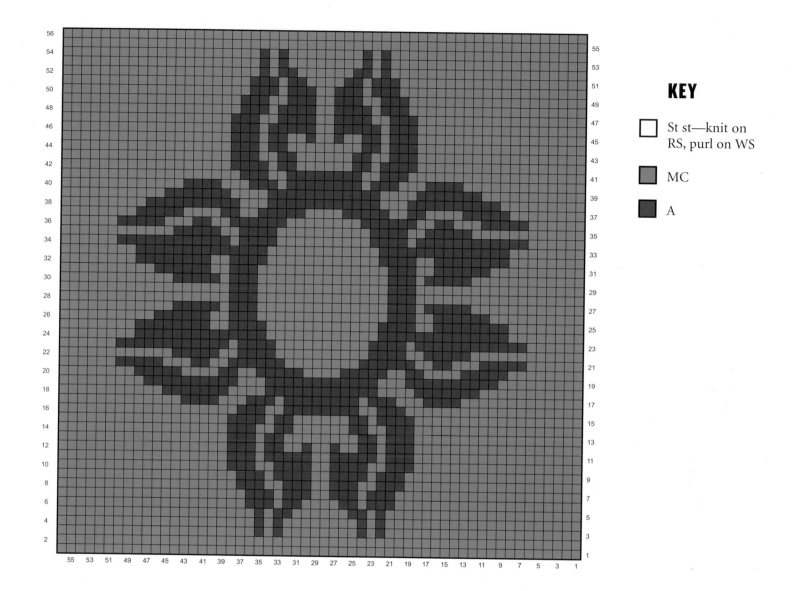

With needle and thread, sew all layered edges together, leaving approximately ¼" (6 mm) selvage. Fold body and strap ends together and sew them in place in same manner. Sew opposite strap side to match the first, 8" (20.3 cm) in length. The end of the sewn seam should be secured with a few back stitches to prevent the seam from coming loose during use. Sew long edges of straps together; remove basting thread.

Notes The fabric chosen for the liner must have enough body to slightly stiffen the bag when assembled, serving a hybrid decorative-functional purpose. You may choose to double a less than sturdy fabric, if necessary—as in our model.

Eve's Garden Cover-up Coat

Had Eve worn this garment back in the day, she might not have gotten into so much trouble. Knit in doubled, four-ply tweed and draped in botanical motifs, this coat features feminine flared hems and a crochetlike lace edging. The clever apple tie detail transforms this piece into a *pièce de resistance*.

Designer: Lisa B. Evans

Sizes

Small (Medium, Large)

Model shown in size Large.

Finished Measurements

Chest: 34 (40, 46)" (86.4 [101.6, 116.8] cm)

Materials
Yarn

Light-weight wool blend

Shown: Rowan Harris 4 Ply (100% wool, 120 yds (109.7 m) / 25 g), #06 Sea Grass (MC) 34 (36, 38 balls); #15 Apple (A), 4 balls; #16 Thistle (B), #18 Thatch (C), #17 Lobster (D), 1 ball each

Needles

Size 8 (5 mm) circular needle, 24" (60 cm) or 29" (74 cm) long; one pair straight needles, 14" (34.4 cm) long, same size; double-pointed needles (5), same size; size 7 (4.5 mm) circular needle, 24" (60 cm) or 29" (74 cm) long; one pair straight needles, 14" (34.4 cm), same size; five double-pointed needles, same size; five size 3 (3.25 mm) double-pointed needles.

Notions

Tapestry needle; stitch marker; 4 cotton balls or small amount of batting; size C/2 (2.75 mm) crochet hook; hook-and-eye closure

Gauge

19 sts and 24 rows = 4" (10 cm) in Stockinette st (St st) with 2 strands of yarn held together.

Notes Due to the large number of sts for the back, it is recommended that you work it back and forth on a circular needle. The body of the jacket is worked with 2 strands of yarn held together, and the lace edgings are worked with 4 strands of yarn held together.

The colorwork shown on the charts is worked as follows: All vines in A are worked using the Fair Isle technique (see page 137); flowers and leaves are worked in duplicate st (see page 143) after the piece is completed. Embellishments such as embroidery stitches can also be added for additional detail to stems and leaves.

Back

With size 7 circular needle and MC, CO 131 (155, 185) sts. (RS) Beg St st. Work even for 6 rows.

Establish Picot Hem

(RS) K1, * k2tog, yo; rep from * to last 2 sts, k2 (turning row). Purl 1 row.

(RS) * K1, p1; rep from * to last st, k1. Purl 1 row, dec 1 (0, 1) sts—130 (155, 184) sts rem.

Begin Chart

(RS) Work Row 1 of chart, beg and end where indicated for your size, and working decs as indicated. Work even until entire chart is complete—76 (90, 104) sts remain. Continuing in MC, work even until piece measures 19¾ (20, 20)" (50 [51, 51] cm) from CO edge, ending on a WS row.

Shape Armholes

(RS) BO 5 (9, 13) sts at beg of next 2 rows—66 (72, 78) sts rem. Work even until armhole measures 9¾ (9¾, 10¼)" (25 [25, 26] cm), ending on a WS row.

Shape Shoulders and Neck

(RS) BO 9 (8, 7) sts, work 13 (12, 11) sts, attach second ball of MC, BO center 22 (32, 42) sts, work to end. Use separate balls of MC and work both sides of neckline at same time. BO 9 (8, 7) sts at beg of next 3 rows and, AT THE SAME TIME, BO 2 sts at each neck edge twice.

Left Front

With size 7 straight needles and MC, CO 77 (91, 105) (RS) Work as for Back for 9 rows. (WS) Purl 1 row, dec 1 st—76 (90, 104) sts rem.

Begin Chart

(RS) Work Row 1 of Chart, beg and end where indicated for your size, and working decs as indicated, CO 7 sts at end of row for facing—

83 (97, 111) sts. (Note: Facing sts are not shown on chart.) (WS) K1, p6, work to end. (RS) Work to last 7 sts, slip 1, k6. Work even as until Chart is complete—48 (57, 67) sts rem. Continuing in MC, work even until armhole measures 8¼ (8, 8½)" (21 [20.3, 21.6] cm), ending on a RS row—43 (48, 54) sts rem.

Shape Shoulders and Neck

BO 14 sts at neck edge once, 3 sts 2 (4, 6) times, 2 sts 0 (1, 2) times, then dec 1 st every other row 5 (4, 4) times and, AT THE SAME TIME, when armhole measures same as for back to shoulder shaping, BO 9 (8, 7) sts at armhole edge twice.

Right Front

Work as for left front, reversing all shaping, and casting on for facing at end of WS row.

Sleeves (make two)

With size 7 needles and MC, CO 75 sts. (WS) Beg St st. Work even for 3 rows.

Establish Picot Hem

(RS) K1, ✳ k2tog, yo; rep from ✳ to last 2 sts, k2 (turning row). Purl 1 row.

(RS) ✳ K1, p1; rep from ✳ to last st, k1. Purl 1 row.

Shape Cuffs

(RS) Continuing in St st, dec 5 sts evenly spaced across row every row 3 times, every 4 rows twice, every 6 rows once, then every 8 rows once—40 sts rem.

Shape Sleeves

(RS) Inc 1 st each edge every other row 5 (6, 12) times, then every 4 rows 19 (18, 14) times—88 (88, 92) sts. Work even until sleeve measures 20½ (21, 21½)" (52.1 [53.3, 54.6] cm) from CO edge, ending on a WS row. BO all sts.

Lace Edging

RS facing, with size 8 straight needles and 4 strands of MC held together, pick up and knit 1 st, ✳ pick up and knit 1 st at each picot point, yo; rep from ✳ to last st, pick up and knit 2 sts—75 sts.

Row 1 K1, ✳ p1, k1; rep from ✳ to end.
Row 2 K1, ✳ k2tog, yo; rep from ✳ end.
Row 3 P1, ✳ k1, p1; rep from ✳ to end.
Row 4 Rep Row 1.
BO all sts purlwise.

Finishing

Block all pieces to measurements. Sew shoulder seams. Sew in sleeves. Sew side and sleeve seams. Turn body and sleeve hems at turning row and sew to WS, being careful not to let sts show on RS. Turn front facings at slip st and sew to WS.

Lace Edging

Body: RS facing, with size 8 circular needle and 4 strands of MC held together, beg at lower left front edge, pick up and knit 1 st, [✳ pick up and knit 1 st at each picot point, yo; rep from ✳ ✳ to side seam, pick up and knit 1 st in side seam] twice; ✳ ✳ pick up and knit 1 st at each picot point, yo; rep from ✳ ✳ to last st, pick up and knit 1 st—279 (331 (389) sts.

Row 1 (WS): K1, ✳ p1, k1; rep from ✳ to end.
Row 2 K1, ✳ k2tog, yo; rep from ✳ to last 2 sts, k2.
Row 3 ✳ P1, k1; rep from ✳ to end.
Row 4 Rep Row 2.
Row 5 Rep Row 1.
Rows 6 and 7 Rep Row 2.
Row 8 K0 (1, 1), ✳ k1, k2tog; rep from ✳ to last 0 (0, 1) st, k0 (0, 1)— 186 (221, 260) sts rem.
BO all sts as follows: K1, k2tog, BO first st, BO to last 3 sts, k2tog k1, BO rem sts.

Collar: RS facing, with size 8 circular needle and 4 strands of MC held together, beg at right front, pick up and knit 19 (23, 28) sts along right front neckline, 21 (27, 33) sts along back neckline, then 19 (23, 28) sts along left front neckline—59 (73, 89) sts.

Row 1 (WS): ✳ K2tog, yo; rep from ✳ to last st, k1.
Row 2 K1, ✳ p1, k1; rep from ✳ to end.
Row 3 K2tog, ✳ [k1, p1] 6 (8, 10) times, k2tog; rep from ✳ to last 1 (1, 3) sts, k1 (1, 3)—54 (67, 82) sts.
Row 4 K2tog, *k1, p1; rep from ✳ to last 3 sts, k0 (1, 0), k2tog—52 (65, 80) sts rem.
Row 5 ✳ K1, p1; rep from ✳ to last 0 (1, 0) st, k1.
BO all sts purlwise.
Block edgings to flatten.

Apple (make 4 in 2 sizes—see below)

With smallest dpn and MC, CO 10 sts loosely.

Row 1 K1–f/b—20 sts.
Rows 2, 6, 8 and 10 Purl.
Row 3 and 11 K2, [k1–f/b, k5] 3 times, k3—23 sts.
Rows 4 and 12 P2, [p2tog, p3] 3 times, p3—20 sts rem.
Rows 5, 7, and 9 Knit.

Row 13 ✳ K2tog; rep from ✳ across—10 sts rem.
Row 14 ✳ P2tog; rep from ✳ across—5 sts rem.

Cut yarn, leaving 12" (30.5 cm) tail. Weave through remaining sts, pull tight and fasten off. Stuff apple with cotton ball or batting. Sew side seam. Thread yarn through middle of the apple and pull tight to create apple core shaping; secure yarn.

Create both large- and small-size apples by using different needle sizes. Work 2 small apples using size 3 dpns and a single strand of MC and 2 large apples using size 8 dpns and 2 strands of D held together.

Leaf (make 2)
With dpn and 2 strands of A held together, CO 5 sts.

Row 1 (RS): K2, yo, k1, yo, k2—7 sts.
Row 2 and all WS rows: Purl.
Row 3 K3, yo, k1, yo, k3— 9 sts.

Row 5 K4, yo, k1, yo, k4—11 sts.
Row 7 Ssk, k7, k2tog—9 sts rem.
Row 9 Ssk, k5, k2tog—7 sts rem.
Row 11 Ssk, k3, k2tog—5 sts rem.
Row 13 Ssk, k1, k2tog—3 sts rem.
Row 15 Sl 1, k2tog, psso—1 st rem.
Fasten off.

Stem
With crochet hook and 2 strands of A held together, work 2 crochet chains 4–5" (10.2–12.7 cm) long, leaving long tail at either end. With tapestry needle, securely attach ends of one chain to two apples. Securely attach chain, at point off-center, to back of one leaf. Attach one side of hook-and-eye-closure to WS of leaf, to the left of center; sew apple and leaf arrangement to right front of jacket just below lace collar. Attach remaining leaf in a slightly offset fashion and sew other side of hook and eye to front of leaf. Attach this arrangement to left front, opposite first side of hook.

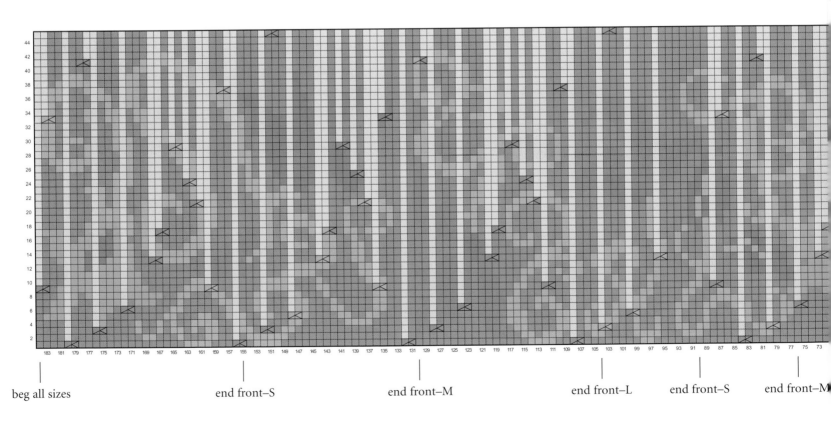

beg all sizes   end front–S   end front–M   end front–L   end front–S   end front–M

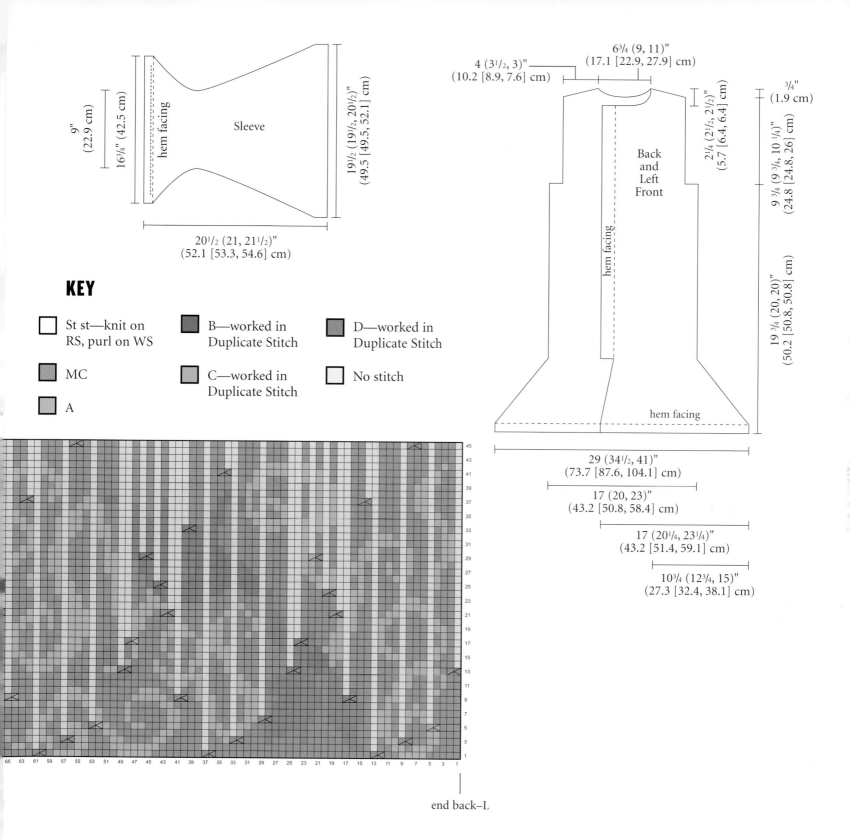

9" (22.9 cm)

16¾" (42.5 cm)

hem facing

Sleeve

19½ (19½, 20½)" (49.5 [49.5, 52.1] cm)

20½ (21, 21½)" (52.1 [53.3, 54.6] cm)

4 (3½, 3)" (10.2 [8.9, 7.6] cm)

6¾ (9, 11)" (17.1 [22.9, 27.9] cm)

¾" (1.9 cm)

2¼ (2½, 2½)" (5.7 [6.4, 6.4] cm)

Back and Left Front

hem facing

9¾ (9¾, 10¼)" (24.8 [24.8, 26] cm)

19¾ (20, 20)" (50.2 [50.8, 50.8] cm)

hem facing

29 (34½, 41)" (73.7 [87.6, 104.1] cm)

17 (20, 23)" (43.2 [50.8, 58.4] cm)

17 (20¼, 23¼)" (43.2 [51.4, 59.1] cm)

10¾ (12¾, 15)" (27.3 [32.4, 38.1] cm)

KEY

- ☐ St st—knit on RS, purl on WS
- ☐ MC
- ☐ A
- ☐ B—worked in Duplicate Stitch
- ☐ C—worked in Duplicate Stitch
- ☐ D—worked in Duplicate Stitch
- ☐ No stitch

end back–L

Fire and Ice Men's Pullover